# Navigating Choppy Waters

*China's Economic Decisionmaking at a Time of Transition*

AUTHORS
Matthew P. Goodman
David A. Parker

*A Report of the CSIS Simon Chair in Political Economy*

***March 2015***

CSIS | CENTER FOR STRATEGIC & INTERNATIONAL STUDIES

ROWMAN & LITTLEFIELD
Lanham • Boulder • New York • London

## About CSIS

For over 50 years, the Center for Strategic and International Studies (CSIS) has worked to develop solutions to the world's greatest policy challenges. Today, CSIS scholars are providing strategic insights and bipartisan policy solutions to help decisionmakers chart a course toward a better world.

CSIS is a nonprofit organization headquartered in Washington, D.C. The Center's 220 full-time staff and large network of affiliated scholars conduct research and analysis and develop policy initiatives that look into the future and anticipate change.

Founded at the height of the Cold War by David M. Abshire and Admiral Arleigh Burke, CSIS was dedicated to finding ways to sustain American prominence and prosperity as a force for good in the world. Since 1962, CSIS has become one of the world's preeminent international institutions focused on defense and security; regional stability; and transnational challenges ranging from energy and climate to global health and economic integration.

Former U.S. senator Sam Nunn has chaired the CSIS Board of Trustees since 1999. Former deputy secretary of defense John J. Hamre became the Center's president and chief executive officer in 2000.

CSIS does not take specific policy positions; accordingly, all views expressed herein should be understood to be solely those of the author(s).



ISBN: 978-1-4422-4078-0 (pb); 978-1-4422-4079-7 (eBook)

Center for Strategic & International Studies
1616 Rhode Island Avenue, NW
Washington, DC 20036
202-887-0200 | www.csis.org

Rowman & Littlefield
4501 Forbes Boulevard
Lanham, MD 20706
301-459-3366 | www.rowman.com

# Contents

# List of Acronyms

| | |
|---|---|
| AIIB | Asian Infrastructure Investment Bank |
| AML | Anti-Monopoly Law |
| APEC | Asia-Pacific Economic Cooperation |
| BIT | Bilateral Investment Treaty |
| CBRC | China Banking Regulatory Commission |
| CCOD | Central Committee Organization Department |
| CCP | Chinese Communist Party |
| CDIC | Central Discipline Inspection Commission |
| CDRLSG | Comprehensively Deepening Reform Leading Small Group |
| CFELSG | Central Finance and Economics Leading Small Group |
| CFIUS | Committee on Foreign Investment in the United States |
| CFWC | Central Financial Work Commission |
| CIRC | China Insurance Regulatory Commission |
| CSRC | China Securities Regulatory Commission |
| CPPCC | Chinese People's Political Consultative Conference |
| FDI | Foreign Direct Investment |
| FTAAP | Free-Trade Area of the Asia-Pacific |
| FTZ | Free-Trade Zone |
| G20 | Group of 20 |
| GDP | Gross Domestic Product |
| IMF | International Monetary Fund |
| ISDS | Investor-State Dispute Settlement |
| JCCT | Joint Commission on Commerce and Trade |
| LSG | Leading Small Group |
| LGFV | Local Government Financing Vehicle |
| MIIT | Ministry of Industry and Information Technology |
| MOF | Ministry of Finance |
| MOFCOM | Ministry of Commerce |
| NDRC | National Development and Reform Commission |
| NSA | National Security Adviser |
| NSC | National Security Council |
| PBOC | People's Bank of China |
| PBSC | Politburo Standing Committee |
| RMB | Renminbi |

| | |
|---|---|
| S&ED | Strategic and Economic Dialogue |
| SAFE | State Administration of Foreign Exchange |
| SHIBOR | Shanghai Interbank Offer Rate |
| SLF | Standing Lending Facility |
| SLO | Standing Liquidity Operations |
| SMEs | Small and Medium-Sized Enterprises |
| SOE | State-Owned Enterprise |
| TPP | Trans-Pacific Partnership |
| UNFCCC | United Nations Framework Convention on Climate Change |
| WTO | World Trade Organization |

# Acknowledgments

This report is the result of a two-year project by the CSIS Simon Chair in Political Economy, with assistance from the CSIS Freeman Chair in China Studies. Through intensive research drawing on primary and secondary materials in Chinese and English, as well as numerous research trips to Beijing, Shanghai, and Hong Kong, roundtables, public events, and over 100 interviews with current and former economic policymakers, academics, think-tank experts, journalists, and other analysts both within and outside China, we sought to analyze and assess the institutions and processes of economic decisionmaking in China at a time of challenging economic and political transition.

The authors are extremely grateful for the invaluable time and insights we received from all of our interlocutors. Special thanks go to the following individuals who met with us several times over the course of the two years and provided critical insights:

Kenneth Lieberthal
Nicholas Lardy
Olin Wethington
Dan Wright
Zhang Bin
Jin Ligang
Barry Naughton
Kevin Nealer
Simon Rabinovitch
Dinny McMahon
Ye Yu
Zhang Haibing
He Fan
David Dollar
Jamil Anderlini
Li Xinxin
William A. Reinsch
Claire Reade

We would like to thank the Smith Richardson Foundation for providing the generous funding that first enabled this project, as well as Alcoa Foundation, the Japan External Trade Relations Organization, and the GE Foundation, whose additional support helped see it through to completion.

The authors would like to acknowledge with appreciation the invaluable assistance of our colleagues at CSIS: Chris Johnson, Freeman Chair in China Studies, for his ever-sharp insights into the dynamics of China's new leadership; Grace Hearty, Simon Chair program manager, for her tireless administrative support; Amy Studdart, Simon Chair deputy director, for her assistance in structuring and reviewing the final report; and Bonnie Glaser and Scott Kennedy of the Freeman Chair for their assistance in its final review; as well as our colleagues in the CSIS Publications Department, led by James Dunton and Alison Bours, for their editing and design work. Any errors that remain are our own.

We would also like to thank CSIS Simon Chair interns Xinyi Yang, Daniel Sofio, Daniel Remler, Alyssa Briggs, Ted Liu, Mikael Lindfors, Zheng Zhu, Laiyin Yuan, and Curtis Yibing Che, all of whom provided able research assistance throughout this project.

# Executive Summary

After 35 years of spectacular growth, the Chinese economy is in a challenging transition. The old model of subsidized finance, massive investment in low-end manufacturing, and export-led growth that propelled China to its current position as the world's second-largest economy is no longer sustainable. Acknowledging a "new normal" of slower growth, Beijing's leadership team of President Xi Jinping and Premier Li Keqiang has put economic reform at the core of their agenda since assuming office in early 2013. By the end of their first year, they had launched an ambitious reform plan designed to rebalance the Chinese economy toward a new consumption-led growth model, with the market playing a "decisive" role in resource allocation.

But despite their predecessors' highly successful management of the economy, it remains to be seen whether China's policymakers today have the "right stuff" to navigate this difficult transition. The economic challenges themselves are of a nature and degree unseen before. Few countries have escaped the so-called middle-income trap that China faces today. The demands on economic policy have burgeoned from a single-minded focus on growth to a multitude of goals including clean air, clean government, and greater equality. Moreover, China's political economy has become increasingly pluralized over the past decade; the range of actors competing to influence economic policy, from state-owned enterprises to environmental activists, has proliferated. All of this makes economic reform both more important and more challenging than at any time since Deng Xiaoping launched the "reform and opening" strategy in 1979.

This project was conceived in response to this uncertainty. Its focus has been on exploring the institutions and processes of economic decisionmaking in China, in an effort to assess the prospects for meaningful reform and a successful transition to a new model of sustainable economic growth. We have put special emphasis on financial reform, both because this is an area of central importance in China's overall reform agenda and because it usefully highlights the institutional dynamics of China's economic decisionmaking. The fundamental question underlying this study is whether China's current economic decisionmakers will be able to steer the world's second-largest economy toward a new model of sustainable growth.

The answer to this question carries enormous significance for the United States. Whether Beijing succeeds or fails in its efforts, China's economic trajectory in coming years will have a substantial impact on the prospects for U.S. and global growth, as well as on broader American interests in the Asia-Pacific region and the world.

After two years of research, our answer to whether China's current crop of policymakers will be able to navigate a challenging economic transition is a qualified yes.

Contrary to initial expectations, Xi Jinping has emerged as the most powerful Chinese leader since Deng Xiaoping. He has demonstrated an impressive command over the levers of power in China's Communist Party–led political system, from personnel to propaganda, as well as a keen sense of political stagecraft. He has reorganized the structure of the Chinese policymaking apparatus to position himself at its apex and center. In November 2013, at the landmark Third Plenum of the 18th Communist Party Central Committee, he put his personal capital behind a sweeping economic and social reform agenda designed to give markets "a decisive role in resource allocation" and to achieve the goal of turning China into a "moderately prosperous society" by 2020.

Through these and other actions, Xi has demonstrated a rapid, opaque, and personalized style of decisionmaking designed to reassert centralized control over economic policymaking and allow experts in Beijing to design and drive a "top-level design" of reform. At the same time, he is using traditional tools of experimentation, incentives to direct local economic actors, and external pressure to advance a comprehensive reform agenda that in many respects echoes successful reform drives of past eras. While there are weaknesses and contradictions in his approach, we assess that Xi's efforts so far have increased the likelihood of achieving the self-declared objective of "major progress" on the ambitious Third Plenum reform agenda by 2020. This is in spite of strong resistance from vested interests and an implementation process that has been uncertain, uncoordinated, and, in many respects, unenthusiastic on the part of the bureaucracy and local governments.

There are risks to this outlook. These range from the potential negative side effects of Xi's centralization of power to the consequences of an intensive anticorruption campaign on the willingness of local officials to implement market-oriented reforms. There is also an underlying tension that animates China's economic reform agenda. The same administration that has proposed giving the market "a decisive role in resource allocation" and is seeking to build an "innovative society" is overseeing the most severe crackdown on the free flow of ideas and information within China in over two decades. It would seem, in other words, that Xi is on track to test whether there truly is a contradiction between authoritarian Party politics and the "modern, harmonious, and creative high-income society" that Beijing hopes to build.

Against this fluid and uncertain backdrop, Washington needs a new mindset in dealing with the China of 2015 and beyond. China poses unique risks, challenges, and opportunities for the United States; no foreign nation will have more impact on U.S. economic, security, and diplomatic interests over coming decades. Accordingly, and in light of the economic decisionmaking dynamics in China described in this study, the report concludes with a dozen specific recommendations for the U.S. government on how best to engage with China on economic issues and how to organize itself better to do so. The starting point is to lead from strength, by getting America's own economic house in order and mobilizing an all-out effort to manage the challenges and opportunities of a rising China.

# 1 Introduction: China's New Economic Navigators

This project began in the spring of 2013, just as China completed its once-in-a-decade leadership transition. As Xi Jinping and Li Keqiang assumed their official roles as president and premier, respectively, it was a time of major economic and political uncertainty.

The previous year, the economy had grown only 7.7 percent in real terms, at the time its lowest rate of expansion since 1999. The Chinese growth model, in the famous words of former premier Wen Jiabao, was "unstable, unbalanced, uncoordinated, and unsustainable."[1] Intensified by an enormous 2009 stimulus package, deployed in response to the global financial crisis, the country's economic imbalances were becoming more apparent by the day: years of overinvestment had led to endemic industrial overcapacity and ghost cities rising up in the midst of deserts; debt levels were exploding, outpacing even the still-breakneck rate of economic growth; and, just as China's working-age population was scheduled to begin a long period of decline, productivity growth was slowing. Despite promises of a managed slowdown, intense anxiety swirled across the pages of the international press, as experts debated whether the world's second-largest economy—and the single-largest driver of global growth for over a decade—might soon face a hard landing.

It was clear that a major economic reform push was essential to securing China's future growth. As a major World Bank study released in 2012 emphasized, without reform China could well find itself stuck in the "middle-income trap," in which the benefits of surplus labor dwindled before China could compete with advanced countries in high-value-added production.[2] To avoid this and address the imbalances described above, Beijing would have to engineer a difficult shift away from the investment- and export-led growth model of the past, and toward a new domestic consumption-led growth model, with the service sector as its primary driver. However, the "soft" reforms required to achieve this—such as modernizing China's regulatory systems and public services, and allowing more market-based

1. "Premier: China confident in maintaining economic growth," Xinhua, March 16, 2007, http://news.xinhuanet.com/english/2007-03/16/content_5856569.htm.

2. World Bank and Development Research Center of the State Council, People's Republic of China, *China 2030: Building a Modern, Harmonious, and Creative Society* (Washington, DC: World Bank, 2013), http://www.worldbank.org/content/dam/Worldbank/document/China-2030-complete.pdf.

resource allocation—were complex, contested, and far reaching. Whether or not China's new leaders would be capable of delivering was far from clear.[3]

Meanwhile, the Bo Xilai scandal that broke in early 2012 marked the most severe political disturbance that the top levels of Communist Party power had seen in decades. Ascending to leadership in the scandal's wake, the Xi-Li duo was widely expected to be handicapped from the start. Not only would Xi and Li be forced to work within the norms of consensus-based decisionmaking that had produced policy paralysis under their predecessors, but in the context of a newly intensified imperative within the party for its leaders to seek stability above all else.

Moreover, Xi and Li entered office facing a more pluralized political economy than any previous generation of Chinese leaders. Hu and Wen had overseen a decade's proliferation of vested interests, from sprawling state-owned firms to corrupt local governments, and the rise of new interest groups, including China's "netizens," industry associations, and environmental activists. All of these actors (and others) had become adept at inserting their interests into the policymaking process, for example, by exploiting cleavages across China's stove-piped state bureaucracy. This had exacerbated China's traditional coordination challenges, and contributed to the policy paralysis of the Hu-Wen era.

The broader array of demands facing Xi and Li reflected this pluralized political economy and illustrated the clear imperative to shift toward a new model of growth. For three and a half decades, growth had provided a unifying goal for Chinese leaders, officials at all levels of government, and the Chinese people to unite around. By 2012, the consequences of China's breakneck development had shattered this consensus. In the face of severe pollution of China's air, soil, and waterways, rising inequality and pervasive local corruption, and a string of high-profile safety scandals over food and consumer goods, the Chinese public had begun to demand more: not only growth, but clean air, clean government, and greater equality. These were goods less easily supplied through quantitative targets and rapid investment. They would require enhancing China's "soft infrastructure," such as its regulatory and public services systems, and overcoming the powerful vested interests that benefited from the status quo. Against this backdrop, prospects for the Xi administration to achieve major reform seemed slim.

Today the picture is markedly different: contrary to almost all initial expectations, Xi Jinping has now emerged as the most powerful Chinese leader since Deng Xiaoping. Demonstrating an impressive command over the levers of party power, from personnel to propaganda, and a keen sense of political stagecraft, Xi has reorganized the structure of the Chinese policymaking apparatus to position himself at its apex and center. In November 2013, at the landmark Third Plenum of the 18th Central Committee of the Chinese Communist Party (CCP), he put forward and personally backed a sweeping reform agenda

3. Dhara Ranasinghe, "Reform With Zeal—Can China's New Leadership Deliver?" CNBC, November 8, 2012, http://www.cnbc.com/id/49705797.

designed to give markets "a decisive role in resource allocation"[4] and achieve the goal of turning China into a "moderately prosperous society."[5] In the same move, he engineered a restructuring of China's economic policymaking apparatus, shifting the locus of decision-making into new party institutions—chaired by Xi and staffed by trusted advisers—and out of the hands of China's gridlocked state bureaucracy. In a further sign of his confidence, conviction, and continued consolidation of power, Xi has also overseen the most intensive and sustained anticorruption drive in over two decades, going so far as to purge from the Communist Party ranks a former member of the elite Politburo Standing Committee, onetime security czar Zhou Yongkang.

None of this guarantees that Xi and China's current policymakers will be able to navigate the economic rapids ahead to deliver a "new normal" of strong, sustainable, and balanced growth.[6] Just as the Third Plenum reform package is impressive in its scope, it is daunting in its technical complexity and sheer ambition. It provides a powerful reminder that for all the rapidity of its ascent on the world stage, China remains very much a developing country in many important respects. It is still struggling to guarantee its people access to such basic goods as safe food and clean water, even as it pursues its vision of creating world-class Chinese companies in sectors from biotechnology to cloud computing.

Moreover, there is a deep tension at the heart of China's economic reform agenda. The same administration that has proposed giving the market "a decisive role in resource allocation" and is seeking to build an "innovative society" is also tightening political control and overseeing the most severe crackdown on the free flow of ideas and information in over two decades. Much hinges on how the current crop of party leaders can manage this fundamental tension, as they continue their pursuit of the "China Dream" of the "great rejuvenation of the Chinese nation."[7]

This project focuses on a small part of this story, but one vital to the future of the whole: the processes and institutions of Chinese economic policymaking. Against the backdrop of a pluralized political economy and facing a broader array of policy objectives, Chinese economic decisionmakers must address a more complex set of challenges than ever before. This report assesses whether the country's decisionmakers, its policymaking processes,

4. For the Chinese-language version of the Third Plenum resolutions, see "授权发布 ：中共中央关于全面深化改革若干重大问题的决定," Xinhua, November 15, 2013, http://news.xinhuanet.com/politics/2013-11/15/c_118164235.htm. For an English translation, see Rogier Creemers, "CCP Central Committee Resolution Concerning Some Major Issues in Comprehensively Deepening Reform," China Copyright and Media, November 15, 2013, https://chinacopyrightandmedia.wordpress.com/2013/11/15/ccp-central-committee-resolution-concerning-some-major-issues-in-comprehensively-deepening-reform/.

5. "Full text of Hu Jintao's report at 18th Party Congress," English.news.cn, November 17, 2012, http://news.xinhuanet.com/english/special/18cpcnc/2012-11/17/c_131981259_4.htm.

6. Xi Jinping first introduced the "new normal" during a May 2014 inspection tour in Henan Province. A Xinhua backgrounder on the subject describes the "new normal" as "not just about speed . . . [but] an improved economic structure which relies more on the tertiary industry and consumption demand, and innovation." From "Xi's 'new normal' theory," Xinhua, November 9, 2014, http://news.xinhuanet.com/english/china/2014-11/09/c_133776839.htm.

7. "Xi pledges 'great renewal of Chinese nation,'" Xinhua, November 29, 2012, http://news.xinhuanet.com/english/china/2012-11/29/c_132008231.htm.

and its institutions—after 35 years of spectacular success—are still well suited to carry out the difficult transition to a new model of strong, sustainable, and balanced growth.

This study is designed to complement the considerable work that many talented analysts have done on China's economic challenges. It does not attempt to provide a quantitative assessment of the Chinese economy's growth trajectory, nor does it focus on the substance of economic reform; instead it explores the institutional dynamics of economic decisionmaking. As China's Communist Party leadership seeks to implement the most ambitious economic reform agenda in decades, these institutional dynamics will play a critical role. Specifically, they will have an important bearing on whether Chinese leaders can implement comprehensive reform without triggering the wracking political and economic instability that so many other developing and transitional economies have endured in the past.

Whether or not China's economic "navigators" can manage this transition will have enormous implications not only for 1.36 billion Chinese but also for the United States. Key U.S. economic and security interests are at stake in China's reform agenda. U.S. growth and employment increasingly depend on the pace and quality of growth in the world's second-largest economy. Moreover, in addition to China's growth, Beijing's approach to economic reform will shape U.S. economic interests and policy responses. For example, greater service sector liberalization and fairer treatment of foreign enterprises will likely strengthen the cooperative aspects of the U.S.-China relationship, while industrial policy, ideological campaigns, and information control will likely fuel the competitive aspects. Beijing's success or failure at economic reform will also inevitably shape its behavior in the Asia-Pacific region and beyond, with important implications for U.S. foreign policy interests.

# 2 China's Economy at an Inflection Point

## The Chinese Economic Miracle

### REFORM AND OPENING, 1978–1989

At the start of "reform and opening" in 1978, China had a gross domestic product (GDP) of only $148.2 billion, and a GDP per capita of $155. By the end of 2013, the Chinese economy was 25 times as large in real terms, and GDP per capita had passed $6,500, placing China within the ranks of upper-middle-income economies.[1] Enabled by a combination of smart politics and favorable economics, this enormous transformation lifted more than 600 million people out of poverty[2] and made China the second-largest economy and single-largest trading nation in the world.

Alongside the structural advantages of cheap labor, high savings and investment rates, and open and expanding export markets, incentives are central to understanding this miraculous growth: it was by craftily aligning China's people and policymakers behind the overarching goal of growth that Deng Xiaoping and his successors made possible the country's miraculous economic transformation.

The first green shoots of a market economy first emerged in the Chinese countryside, following the landmark Third Plenum of the 11th Central Committee of the CCP in 1978.[3] Previously, the Chinese state and economy were inseparable: guided by broad five-year plans developed by the State Planning Commission, the government determined the allocation of resources, set production quotas, and managed the distribution of goods. At the Third Plenum, the decision was made to "give farmers a chance to catch their breath" by reducing overambitious production targets, which, accompanied by an overall relaxing of

1. These figures are from the World Bank's "World Development Indicators" and are calculated in current U.S. dollars. The World Bank DataBank, http://databank.worldbank.org/data/home.aspx.

2. World Bank, "Results Profile: China Poverty Reduction," March 19, 2010, http://www.worldbank.org/en/news/feature/2010/03/19/results-profile-china-poverty-reduction.

3. This change was not immediate, nor did the plenum mark the decisive shift toward a greater role for the market with which it is often credited. The actual process of introducing the early reforms was uncertain and incremental. See Chris Buckley, "Portrait of Deng as Reformer in 1978 Plenum Ignores History," *New York Times*, November 9, 2013, http://sinosphere.blogs.nytimes.com/2013/11/09/portrait-of-deng-as-reformer-in-1978-plenum-ignores-history/.

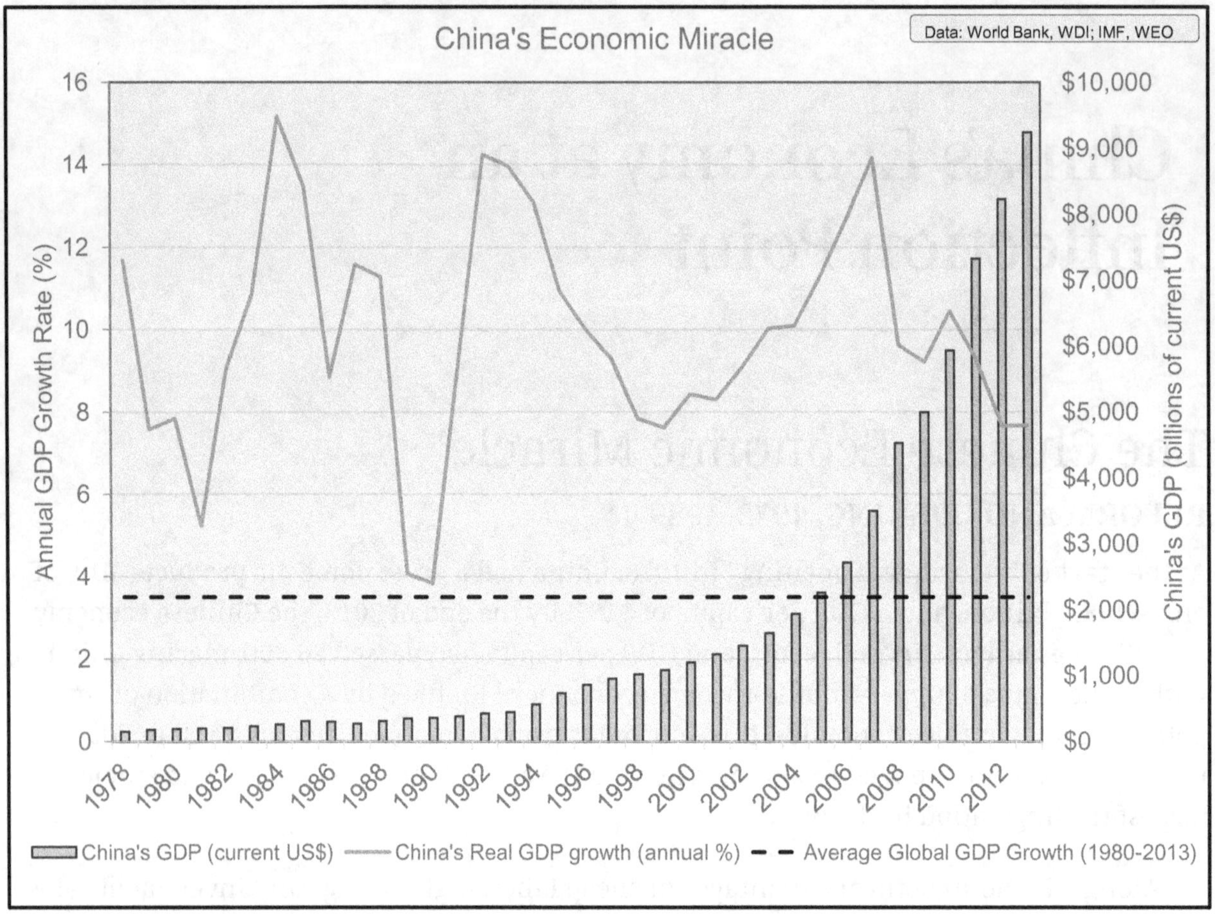


the political environment, created new opportunities for local experimentation.[4] Such experimentation eventually gave rise to the famous "household responsibility system," which allowed farmers to manage individual plots of land and to sell at market rates what they produced in excess of official targets. Where Beijing's earlier exhortations to produce for the sake of plans had failed to spur the desired burst in grain production, the introduction of even these modest market incentives succeeded in stimulating a revolution in Chinese agricultural productivity.

Improvements in Chinese agricultural productivity also had the side effect of freeing up labor in the countryside to engage in other forms of economic activity, leading to a proliferation of locally run factories (referred to as township and village enterprises). Operating outside of the dictates of China's central planners, these factories created vital competition for inefficient state-owned enterprises (SOEs), in addition to meeting unmet market demands. Accompanied by increased openness to foreign investment, the result was that China began to rapidly "grow out of the plan." From 1980 to 1988, the Chinese economy averaged 10.4 percent annual GDP growth, more than doubling its size in less

4. This account draws heavily from the work of Barry Naughton. Barry Naughton, *The Chinese Economy: Transitions and Growth* (Cambridge, MA: MIT Press, 2006), 88–90.

than a decade.[5] Over the same period, the Chinese government downsized significantly, with the number of state agencies reduced from 100 to 60.[6]

Of course, this simple narrative overstates the stability of China's political and macro economy during this period. Growth and inflation fluctuated enormously, while the process of reform moved in fits and starts. At the time, Chinese leaders were not only grappling with the issue of how to manage a gradual and piecemeal reduction of the central government's control over the economy, but debating among themselves the extent to which it was appropriate or desirable to do so. A major landmark was reached in 1987 at the 13th Party Congress, when the party formally recognized the private sector as a "necessary supplement" to the public sector. This demonstrated a major shift in consciousness among party elites regarding the proper relationship between state, party, and economy. For the first time, Chinese leaders made the key determination that diminishing the role of state and party in the economy was necessary. The shift in awareness led to 1988 legislation that separated corporate and government management structures for the first time—arguably the most important reform of this period.

## FROM THE SOUTHERN TOUR TO THE 18TH PARTY CONGRESS, 1989–2012

Events in Tiananmen Square in 1989 brought this revolution to a screeching halt, leading to the ouster of then general secretary Zhao Ziyang and reempowering conservative elements within the Communist Party.[7] The contemporaneous collapse of the Soviet Union spurred a tense debate over whether reform could save the party or would destroy it, leading conservatives to aggressively reassert their control over the economy and the central planning bureaucracy. This spurred Deng Xiaoping's famous "Southern Tour" in 1992, on which he highlighted the tremendous boom taking place in coastal "special economic zones." While successful in marginalizing the ideological opponents of reform, the Southern Tour also saw Deng further devolve authority to the provinces, which would pose challenges later as they functionally came to resemble independent fiefdoms more than extensions of the central authorities.

Deng's gambit freed the 14th Party Congress to officially endorse a "socialist market economy" in 1992 and announce its intention to create a modern corporate system, priming the pump for a decade of reforms under Zhu Rongji (first as vice premier from 1993 to 1998, later as premier from 1998 to 2003). Major impetus and direction for reform also came from external sources, as China sought accession to the World Trade Organization (WTO). This reflected the view among Chinese leaders during this period that economic growth was the condition for continued party rule, and would be best sustained by increased competition through integration with the global economy.[8] In 1994, the government

---

5. International Monetary Fund (IMF), *World Economic Outlook: Legacies, Clouds, Uncertainties* (Washington, DC: IMF, October 2014), https://www.imf.org/external/pubs/ft/weo/2014/02/pdf/text.pdf.

6. Organization for Economic Cooperation and Development (OECD), *Governance in China* (Paris: OECD, September 2005), http://www.oecd.org/gov/governanceinchina.htm.

7. Naughton, *The Chinese Economy*, 98–100.

8. Nicholas R. Lardy, "Issues in China's WTO Accession" (speech before the U.S.-China Security Review Commission, May 9, 2001), http://www.brookings.edu/research/testimony/2001/05/09foreignpolicy-lardy.

passed major reforms to simplify China's foreign exchange regime and establish a degree of current account convertibility, accompanied by a devaluation of its currency, the renminbi (RMB).[9] While these reforms were intended as an immediate precursor to WTO membership, the process of accession ultimately took nearly a decade, finally reaching completion in December 2001.

During this period, Zhu Rongji used the WTO as a club to beat back vested interests and drive the reform process forward. Simultaneously, he fought to further disentangle the state from the economy through an enormous downsizing of the bureaucracy and state-owned sector. Over the course of the decade ending in 2003, public enterprise employment declined by more than 40 percent, or nearly 50 million workers.[10] In addition, Zhu, with the support of the then general secretary Jiang Zemin, oversaw a major overhaul of the Chinese tax system, pushed for more coherent national regulatory policies, and implemented dramatic and far-reaching reforms of the financial system. As a result, the Chinese economy was positioned for a decade of breakneck expansion at the end of Zhu's tenure: further spurred by China's WTO accession and positive external conditions, real GDP growth averaged 10.6 percent annually from 2003 to 2012.

At the same time, Chinese society had been exhausted by the pace and extent of the Zhu-era reforms, and the next generation of Chinese leaders took note. In response, the leadership duo of President Hu Jintao and Premier Wen Jiabao centered its policy agenda on the promotion of a "harmonious society," seeking to improve social welfare and narrow urban-rural and coastal-inland wealth disparities.[11] Not only did this strategy fail in its stated aims, but these and other policies pursued by the Hu-Wen leadership also ended up empowering a new breed of SOEs[12] and failed to prevent the continued weakening of central control over provincial governments. This trend deepened with the onset of the global financial crisis, which forced Beijing to announce a $586 billion (RMB 4 trillion) stimulus package in November 2008. While successful in arresting the economy's free fall, the stimulus not only exacerbated China's overreliance on investment-led growth but also further entrenched the aforementioned vested interests. By the end of the Hu-Wen leadership's decade in power three years later, a new approach was necessary.

9. The official name of China's currency is the renminbi. It is counted in units of yuan and is often referred to as such.

10. Kevin Hamlin and Scott Lanman (ed.), "Li's Shock Treatment to China Lenders Evokes Ex-Reformer," Bloomberg, June 26, 2013, http://www.bloomberg.com/news/articles/2013-06-26/li-s-shock-treatment-to-china-lenders-evokes-ex-reformer.

11. Kin-man Chan, "Harmonious Society," in *International Encyclopedia of Civil Society*, ed. Helmut K. Anheier and Stefan Toepler (New York: Springer, 2009), https://www.cuhk.edu.hk/centre/ccss/publications/km_chan/CKM_14.pdf.

12. Some analysis has questioned conventional wisdom regarding China's SOEs having become more empowered during the Hu-Wen period. For the most thorough critique of this view, see Nicholas R. Lardy, *Markets Over Mao: The Rise of Private Business in China*, Peterson Institute for International Economics, September 10, 2014.

## The Need for a New Growth Model

As the Xi administration took office, two things were clear: China had reached the end of its old growth model, and the days of double-digit growth were over.[13] In a 2012 report coauthored with the Development Research Center of the State Council, the World Bank cautioned, "The opportunities and challenges in the next two decades will be unlike those [China has] encountered in the past and will demand a new development strategy."[14] These echoed the less diplomatic words of the then premier Wen, who had argued since 2007 that China's growth was "unstable, unbalanced, uncoordinated, and unsustainable."[15]

Under Hu and Wen, China relied on external demand to propel its growth, using an array of explicit and hidden subsidies—including an undervalued currency—to boost exports and suppress imports. The result was massive current account surpluses and accumulation of over $3.5 trillion in foreign-exchange reserves. Since the global financial crisis of 2008–2009, as advanced economies struggled to grow, Chinese leaders opted to use public investment to take up the slack. Artificially low deposit rates and a lack of social protections forced Chinese consumers to save excessively,[16] while state banks used these funds to provide cheap capital to poorly run SOEs.[17] These companies then overinvested in unproductive assets, on average providing a negative 6.29 percent return on equity.[18] The state firms (in conjunction with local governments) also used their access to cheap credit to pursue speculative investments in the real estate sector, fueling property bubbles in major municipalities and unsustainable property booms in minor ones.

By 2012, China had been investing more than 40 percent of its GDP per year for a decade.[19] Consumption as a share of GDP had fallen from 42 percent in 2003 to 35 percent in 2012—roughly 20 percent lower than in a typical emerging market economy.[20] The industrial sector, which benefited from below-market prices for capital, land, energy, and other

---

13. World Bank and Development Research Center of the State Council, People's Republic of China, *China 2030: Building a Modern, Harmonious, and Creative Society* (Washington, DC: World Bank, 2013), http://www.worldbank.org/content/dam/Worldbank/document/China-2030-complete.pdf.

14. Ibid.

15. "Premier: China confident in maintaining economic growth," Xinhua, March 16, 2007, http://news.xinhuanet.com/english/2007-03/16/content_5856569.htm.

16. The reasons underpinning China's high household savings rates are much debated, and deposit rate controls are not the only factor. For example, Liu (2014) estimates that job uncertainty resulting from market-based reforms accounted for about a third of Chinese urban household wealth accumulation from 1995 to 2002. Another key factor is China's relatively threadbare social safety net. For more, see Zheng Liu, "Job Uncertainty and Chinese Household Savings," Federal Reserve Bank of San Francisco, February 3, 2014, http://www.frbsf.org/economic-research/publications/economic-letter/2014/february/job-uncertainty-china-household-savings-state-owned-enterprises-iron-rice-bowl/.

17. Nicholas R. Lardy, *Sustaining China's Economic Growth after the Financial Crisis* (Washington, DC: Peterson Institute for International Economics, 2012).

18. Hong Sheng and Nong Zhao, *China's State-Owned Enterprises: Nature, Performance and Reform* (Singapore: World Scientific, 2012).

19. IMF, "People's Republic of China: 2012 Article IV Consultation," IMF Country Report No. 12/195, July 2012, https://www.imf.org/external/pubs/ft/scr/2012/cr12195.pdf.

20. Nicholas R. Lardy and Nicholas Borst, "A Blueprint for Rebalancing the Chinese Economy," Peterson Institute for International Economics Policy Brief no. 13-2, February 2013, http://www.iie.com/publications/pb/pb13-2.pdf.

resources, was overdeveloped and overcapacity. The services sector was its mirror image. A host of factors, from excessive regulations and administrative monopolies to weak intellectual property rights protection and repressed domestic consumption, had left services industries severely underdeveloped for a country of China's income level. To unlock a new model of consumption- and services-led growth, the new leaders would have to rectify these imbalances, modernize the "soft infrastructure" of regulations and institutions, and overcome the powerful vested interests that had benefited from the status quo.

They would have to do so in the context of a secular economic slowdown. The size of China's working-age population had begun to decline and the country was entering a period of rapid aging. The major gains from reallocating labor from agricultural to industrial activities had already been realized. By moving ever closer to the technological frontier, China had achieved dramatic productivity gains, but also become a victim of its own success. Future gains would require an ever more skilled labor force and the master of ever more sophisticated technologies. And even in the best-case scenarios projected at the time, this transition would still see China's growth rate moderate to around 5 percent by the mid-2020s.[21]

At the same time, the negative consequences of China's breakneck development had undermined the consensus surrounding growth as a national project. Land seizures used by cash-strapped local governments to raise revenue and fund growth-boosting local investment had become a source of social unrest. Income inequality had risen sharply nationwide and deepened the divide between inland provinces and richer coastal areas, between urban and rural citizens, and even within cities.[22] Industrial activity had tainted China's arable land and waterways, while high concentrations of airborne particulate routinely produced choking haze and grounded flights along the coast.[23] A parade of high-profile corruption investigations, pervasive local corruption, and scandals involving everything from tainted infant formula[24] to disastrous train crashes had undermined public trust in government.[25]

As the First Plenum of the 18th CCP Central Committee drew to a close in November 2012 and the new seven-member Politburo Standing Committee (PBSC) was revealed, few

---

21. For a fuller description of these and other challenges facing the Chinese economy at the time, see World Bank and Development Research Center of the State Council, People's Republic of China, *China 2030*.

22. For an overview of some of the sources and dimensions of Chinese economic inequality, see Martin King Whyte, "China's Post-Socialist Inequality," in *Current History* 111, no. 746 (September 2012), http://scholar.harvard.edu/files/martinwhyte/files/whyte-current_history.pdf; and Nan Wu, "Income inequality in China and the urban-rural divide," Journalist's Resource, August 19, 2014, http://journalistsresource.org/studies/international/china/income-inequality-todays-china.

23. Bloomberg, "Beijing 'barely suitable' for life as heavy pollution shrouds China's capital," *Sydney Morning Herald*, February 26, 2014, http://www.smh.com.au/environment/beijing-barely-suitable-for-life-as-heavy-pollution-shrouds-chinas-capital-20140225-33ghq.html; Penny Ping and Gregory Turk, "Xi Jinping Calls Pollution Beijing's Biggest Challenge," Bloomberg, February 27, 2014, http://www.bloomberg.com/news/articles/2014-02-26/xi-calls-pollution-beijing-s-biggest-challenge-as-smog-eases.

24. "Formula for disaster," *The Economist*, September 18, 2008, http://www.economist.com/node/12262271.

25. Evan Osnos, "Boss Rail," *New Yorker*, October 22, 2012, http://www.newyorker.com/magazine/2012/10/22/boss-rail.

predicted a decisive transition was imminent. Xi and his fellow members of the CCP's fifth-generation leadership were seeking to reform an economy that had more than quadrupled in size since the start of the last major reform push in 1998. Moreover, they faced a more pluralized policy environment than any Chinese leaders before them. Influential SOEs, large private-sector actors, empowered provincial leaders, fractious government ministries, and a more vocal civil society were all competing intensely to influence policy—and doing so through a host of ever more sophisticated techniques and technologies.[26] To many longtime observers, it seemed an economic crisis was inevitable, if not imminent.[27]

## The Third Plenum Reform Agenda

On November 12, 2013, the 18th Central Committee released a brief communiqué summarizing the resolution endorsed at its just-concluded Third Plenum. Analysts panned the document for its vague language, lack of detail, and overall failure to meet expectations stoked by months of promises of "unprecedented" reforms.[28] As one veteran analyst explained to this study's authors that night in Beijing, "this is beyond disappointing—there is nothing here." Chinese stocks fell on its release.[29]

This assessment proved premature.[30] Two days later, the full Decision of the Central Committee of the Communist Party of China on Some Major Issues Concerning Comprehensively Deepening Reform (henceforth the "Decision") was released, alongside a detailed explanation from Xi Jinping himself. The Decision and Xi's accompanying explanation highlighted a major theoretical achievement, the upgrading of the market's role in resource allocation from "basic" to "decisive"—a move described by Nicholas Lardy, a veteran analyst of the Chinese economy, as "potentially revolutionary."[31] Beneath this bold headline commitment was what economist Barry Naughton has described as the economic

---

26. For fuller accounts of some of the ways in which new actors are entering into China's economic policymaking process, see Scott Kennedy, "Comparing Formal and Informal Lobbying Practices in China," *China Information*, July 2009, http://chinatrack.typepad.com/files/Kennedy_%20Comparing_CI_PUB_July_09.pdf; Andrew Mertha, *China's Water Warriors: Citizen Action and Policy Change* (Ithaca, NY: Cornell University Press, 2010).

27. For example, see James McGregor, *No Ancient Wisdom, No Followers: The Challenges of Chinese Authoritarian Capitalism* (Westport, CT: Prospecta Press, 2012); Chris Buckley, "China must reform or risk crisis, experts warn new leader," Reuters, October 7, 2012, http://www.reuters.com/article/2012/10/07/us-china-politics-reform-idUSBRE8960K320121007.

28. Megha Rajagopalan and Michael Perry, ed., "China leader promises 'unprecedented' reforms at key Party meeting," Reuters, October 26, 2013, http://www.reuters.com/article/2013/10/26/us-china-reforms-plenum-idUSBRE99P02220131026.

29. Mamta Badkar, "The Shanghai Composite Took a Beating after China's Big Meeting on Reforms," *Business Insider*, November 13, 2013, http://www.businessinsider.com/shanghai-composite-falls-after-3rd-plenum-2013-11.

30. Christopher K. Johnson, "China Announces Sweeping Reform Agenda at Plenum," CSIS, November 15, 2013, http://csis.org/publication/china-announces-sweeping-reform-agenda-plenum.

31. Nicholas Lardy (remarks at "Deciphering China's Third Plenum: Politics, Policy, and Prospects," CSIS, Washington, DC, November 22, 2013), http://csis.org/event/deciphering-chinas-third-plenum-politics-policy-and-prospects.

equivalent of "shock and awe," a comprehensive "vision statement with a to-do list" for the next stage of China's reform and opening.[32]

Across 60 articles and the 336 specific reform measures covered therein, the Decision delivered on PBSC member Yu Zhengsheng's pre-plenum promise that reforms would be "unprecedented and will promote profound changes in every area of the economy and society."[33] An extensive Asia Society report on the plan groups the reforms into nine major substantive categories under the overarching theme of redefining the role of government in the Chinese economy: center-local fiscal reform; competition policy reform; financial system reform; foreign trade and investment reform; state-owned enterprise reform; land policy rationalization; labor and shared welfare; environmental policy reform; and innovation policy reform.[34] This extensive agenda sent a strong signal that China's leaders grasped the challenges facing the economy and were committed to addressing them.

The outcomes from the Third Plenum also signaled Xi Jinping's growing authority within the Chinese political system. While the Decision was a consensus document officially endorsed by the full Central Committee, Xi's accompanying explanation of its contents[35] (along with detailed accounts of his involvement in the drafting process released by official media outlets) showed his intent to personally brand the agenda. Xi's role was further highlighted in the Decision's announcement that he would head a new "leading small group" (discussed in more detail below) to oversee the implementation of reform. The creation of this new body demonstrated that Xi had the clout to create structural solutions at the highest levels of decisionmaking to get around the gridlock and stovepiping of China's state bureaucracy.

Policymaking takes place in three broad stages: problem identification, policy generation, and policy implementation. The Third Plenum showed that China's leaders had successfully navigated this first stage and possessed a firm grasp of the country's economic challenges. Furthermore, the Decision illustrated that Beijing was at least partway through the process of policy generation: a "vision statement" for reform was evident, even if clear priorities and the promulgation of specific metrics and regulations remained to be completed. The major question remaining was implementation, and whether or not the Chinese economic policymaking apparatus would be up for the challenge of pushing through reforms in a more pluralized political economy.

---

32. Barry Naughton, "After the Third Plenum: Economic Reform Revival Moves toward Implementation," *China Leadership Monitor*, no. 43 (Spring 2014), http://www.hoover.org/sites/default/files/uploads/documents/CLM43BN.pdf.

33. Wenxin Fan, "China Signals 'Unprecedented' Changes on Agenda at Plenum," Bloomberg, October 28, 2013, http://www.bloomberg.com/news/articles/2013-10-27/china-signals-unprecedented-policy-changes-on-agenda-at-plenum.

34. Daniel H. Rosen, *Avoiding the Blind Alley* (Washington, DC: Asia Society Policy Institute, 2014), http://asiasociety.org/policy-institute/china-economy.

35. "Xi explains China's reform plan," Xinhua, November 15, 2013, http://news.xinhuanet.com/english/china/2013-11/15/c_132891949.htm.

# 3 China's Economic Policymaking Apparatus

Almost 40 years after Mao Zedong's death, the Chinese economic policymaking apparatus reflects as much his legacy as that of Deng Xiaoping. Indeed, to ignore the extent of continuity across the eras that these two leaders defined is to miss much of what drives and is distinctive to China's economic policymaking process and system. This is of particular importance given the fluidity of the formal institutions of the Chinese policymaking apparatus. Over nearly four decades of rapid growth, these have been constantly reformed and rearranged to address the needs of a modernizing economy. They have also been adjusted to serve successive generations of Chinese leaders' policymaking styles, preferences, and political circumstances—meaning that a narrow focus on formal lines of authority almost invariably misses the true centers of power and decisionmaking.

The most important enduring characteristic that links the eras of Mao and Deng and persists through the present is, of course, the centrality of the CCP. In the words of one Chinese professor at a prominent Beijing university, "The Party is like God. He is everywhere. You just can't see him."[1] Over the course of reform and opening, the extent of the party's involvement in day-to-day economic decisionmaking has swelled and shrunk in cycles. On balance, it has gradually ceded to the market a more important role in resource allocation and given the formal state apparatus greater responsibility for day-to-day administration of economic affairs. However, the CCP continues to define the context within which economic policymaking takes place. Its enduring goals as a political entity—maintaining CCP rule and achieving the "great rejuvenation of the Chinese nation"—together with the underlying realities of China's vast and varied geography and enormous population, have in turn shaped the dominant features that characterize the structure of China's economic policymaking apparatus and its manner of operation through the present.

Chinese economic decisionmaking and the policymaking apparatus are characterized by contradictions. It is no accident that the Chinese system has been described as both "fragmented" and "authoritarian" for over two decades.[2] Such contradictions reflect the

1. Quoted in Richard McGregor, *The Party: The Secret World of China's Communist Rulers* (New York: Harper Perennial, 2012), 1.

2. The most popular and enduring model of the Chinese political system is the "fragmented authoritarianism" model put forward by Michel Oksenberg and Kenneth Lieberthal in 1988, which has continued to influence much of the academic discussion of China's political system through the present. See Kenneth Lieberthal

vast array of forces at work in China's modern political economy, many of which tug in opposite directions. Just as the party exerts a strong general pressure toward the centralization of policymaking, China's sheer size and the diversity of local interests exert an opposing force in favor of greater decentralization. Successive generations of Chinese leaders have extended the economic miracle of the past 35 years by accommodating these pressures through policies that satisfied both the political and economic imperatives of each moment. The particular challenge of the present is that the objectives of policy have become diffuse, and growth no longer provides a unifying force and clear direction for economic policy.

The remainder of this chapter describes the major structural characteristics of the Chinese economic policymaking apparatus. It first reviews the structure of the Communist Party and the functions of key party organs. A second section examines the state apparatus, with attention to the structure and roles of both the central and local governments. The final section reviews major structural changes to the institutions of Chinese economic policymaking that have been introduced under the Xi administration.[3]

# The Communist Party

At 86.7 million members, the CCP is the world's largest Communist party. If it remains in power through 2019, it will also be the longest-ruling Communist party in history. Although its membership accounts for only about 6 percent of China's total population, the CCP dominates Chinese society and permeates the formal apparatus of government. At its heart, the CCP is a Leninist system: structured to ensure central control of the major levers of power (including most especially arms, personnel, and propaganda) and to limit opportunities for horizontal collaboration that could threaten central control.

The CCP is led from the top down, starting with the seven-member Standing Committee of the Politburo of the 18th Central Committee (more commonly referred to as the Politburo Standing Committee, or PBSC). These seven leaders concurrently sit on the full Politburo, which has 25 members and is next in terms of functional authority. Politburo members are in turn part of the larger Central Committee, a body made up of 205 full members and 171 alternate members. The Central Committee meets at least once every year in plenary sessions. The documents endorsed at these meetings are among the CCP's most authoritative statements of policy.

The CCP's presence in the institutions of state and society is extensive. Almost every high-ranking state official is additionally a party member and required to participate in party activities, such as periodically organized nationwide study campaigns. Party

---

and Michel Oksenberg, *Policy Making in China: Leaders, Structures, and Processes* (Princeton, NJ: Princeton University Press, 1988).

3. As the focus of this report is on economic policymaking, it does not cover in depth many aspects of the Chinese political cycle. For a further discussion of this, and other features of the Chinese political system, see Susan V. Lawrence and Michael F. Martin, "Understanding China's Political System," Congressional Research Service, March 20, 2013, https://www.fas.org/sgp/crs/row/R41007.pdf.

committees exist in every ministry, at all levels of government, in universities and unions, and in public and private companies throughout China—including many foreign enterprises. Most senior SOE managers are party members and are linked to their counterparts in the government and party via a network of secure red phones.[4] Even outside of formal party channels, officially sanctioned organizations, such as the Chinese People's Political Consultative Conference (CPPCC)[5] and party-approved unions and trade federations,[6] provide a further means of monitoring and co-opting groups not directly under the CCP umbrella.

In addition, the party has its own specialized organs that control key levers of power, such as personnel appointments, propaganda, and anticorruption investigations. These institutions are typically cloned at all government levels. Some key institutions include the following:

*Central Committee Organization Department (CCOD)*: The CCOD oversees administration of the party's central *nomenklatura* system, which controls appointments to the top several thousand positions in the party, state, and other relevant organizations. It also has responsibilities for party member recruitment, performance evaluation, investigation, and training.

*Central Discipline Inspection Commission (CDIC)*: Party officials are officially subject to the party's discipline and can only be prosecuted for violations of Chinese law if they are first expelled from the party. The CDIC is the party's powerful internal antigraft body, though its remit extends beyond anticorruption. It is also responsible for ensuring that party officials maintain ideological discipline. The current head of the CDIC is Wang Qishan, China's former financial policy czar and a member of the PBSC.[7]

Although the party has delegated much of the authority for day-to-day administration of economic affairs to the state apparatus, a key channel for its continued oversight and management is secretive, high-level party committees known as "leading small groups" (LSGs). The relevant body for economic affairs has long been the Central Finance and

4. McGregor, *The Party*, 8–10.

5. The CPPCC is a political advisory body overseen by the United Front Work Department of the CCP. Delegates include members of China's officially recognized non-Communist parties, unions, trade federations, minority groups, and other segments of Chinese society. Local branches of the CPPCC exist in all jurisdictions down to the county level.

6. For example, the All-China Federation of Trade Unions. For a fuller treatment of trade unions and government-business relations in China, see Scott Kennedy, *The Business of Lobbying in China* (Cambridge, MA: Harvard University Press, 2005).

7. For a discussion of the evolution of the CDIC, see Guo Yong, "The Evolvement of the Chinese Communist Party Discipline Inspection Commission in the Reform Era," *China Review* 12, no. 1 (Spring 2012), http://connection.ebscohost.com/c/articles/74698354/evolvement-chinese-communist-party-discipline-inspection-commission-reform-era. For a discussion of its current workings, see William Wan, "Secretive agency leads most intense anti-corruption effort in modern Chinese history," *Washington Post*, July 2, 2014, http://www.washingtonpost.com/world/asia_pacific/secretive-agency-leads-most-intense-anti-corruption-effort-in-modern-chinese-history/2014/07/02/48aff932-cf68-11e3-937f-d3026234b51c_story.html.

Economics Leading Small Group (CFELSG), which has operated continuously since March 1980.[8]

The exact role of the CFELSG (and other LSGs) has not been consistent across different generations of leadership. Instead, the CFELSG's function has varied depending on the preferences and style of the leaders at the time. However, in general, the CFELSG's role is to provide a venue for bringing together top-level leaders to coordinate and reach consensus on key economic issues. Like each permanent LSG, which has a small general office located within a party, government, or military agency that carries out the day-to-day work of managing paper flow, drafting documents, and coordinating across the relevant aspects of the policymaking apparatus, the CFELSG has its own general office.[9] The staffing of this office has reportedly been expanding under Xi Jinping.

## The State Council

Although the party has consistently maintained a "leading role" in setting China's economic policy priorities, the state manages most day-to-day administration of economic affairs. At the top of China's governmental policymaking hierarchy is the State Council, effectively China's cabinet. The State Council and its ministries directly issue many of the regulations that govern the Chinese economy, though major legislation[10] formally requires the approval of the National People's Congress (NPC), China's legislature.[11] While China is formally a unitary country in terms of administration, the policymaking apparatus is in fact extremely decentralized, as discussed below.

The full State Council has 35 members: the premier, four vice premiers,[12] and five state councilors[13]—who together comprise the executive committee—and 25 heads of ministry-

---

8. Alice Miller, "The CCP Central Committee's Leading Small Groups," *China Leadership Monitor*, no. 26 (Fall 2008), http://www.hoover.org/sites/default/files/uploads/documents/CLM26AM.pdf.

9. For more extensive coverage of these bodies, see Carol Lee Hamrin, "The Party Leadership System" in *Bureaucracy, Politics, and Decision-making in Post-Mao China*, ed. Kenneth G. Lieberthal and David M. Lampton (Berkeley: University of California Press, 1992); Alice Miller, "The CCP Central Committee's Leading Small Groups," *China Leadership Monitor*, no. 26 (Fall 2008), http://www.hoover.org/sites/default/files/uploads/documents/CLM26AM.pdf; and Alice Miller, "More Already on the Central Committee's Leading Small Groups," *China Leadership Monitor*, no. 44 (Summer 2014), http://www.hoover.org/sites/default/files/research/docs/clm44am.pdf.

10. For a description of the major categories of legislation in the Chinese system, see appendix III in Nathaniel Ahrens, *China's Industrial Policymaking Process* (Washington, DC: CSIS, January 2013), http://csis.org/files/publication/130124_Ahrens_ChinaPolicymaking_Web.pdf.

11. The NPC is formally the "highest organ of state power," authorized to approve the annual budget and to appoint or remove state leaders. Functionally, however, the NPC has little power and almost always votes in favor of state proposals. See Susan V. Lawrence and Michael F. Martin, "Understanding China's Political System," Congressional Research Service, March 20, 2013, https://www.fas.org/sgp/crs/row/R41007.pdf.

12. Vice Premier Zhang Gaoli is frequently referred to as the "executive vice premier." While this is not a title used in official Chinese media, it reflects Zhang's position as both a vice premier and a member of the top-ranked PBSC (see below).

13. State councilors frequently serve in multiple positions simultaneously. For example, State Councilor Yang Jing serves concurrently as the State Council secretary-general and as president of the Chinese Academy of Governance (among other positions). State Councilors Guo Shengkun and Chang Wanquan serve concurrently as ministers of public security and national defense, respectively.

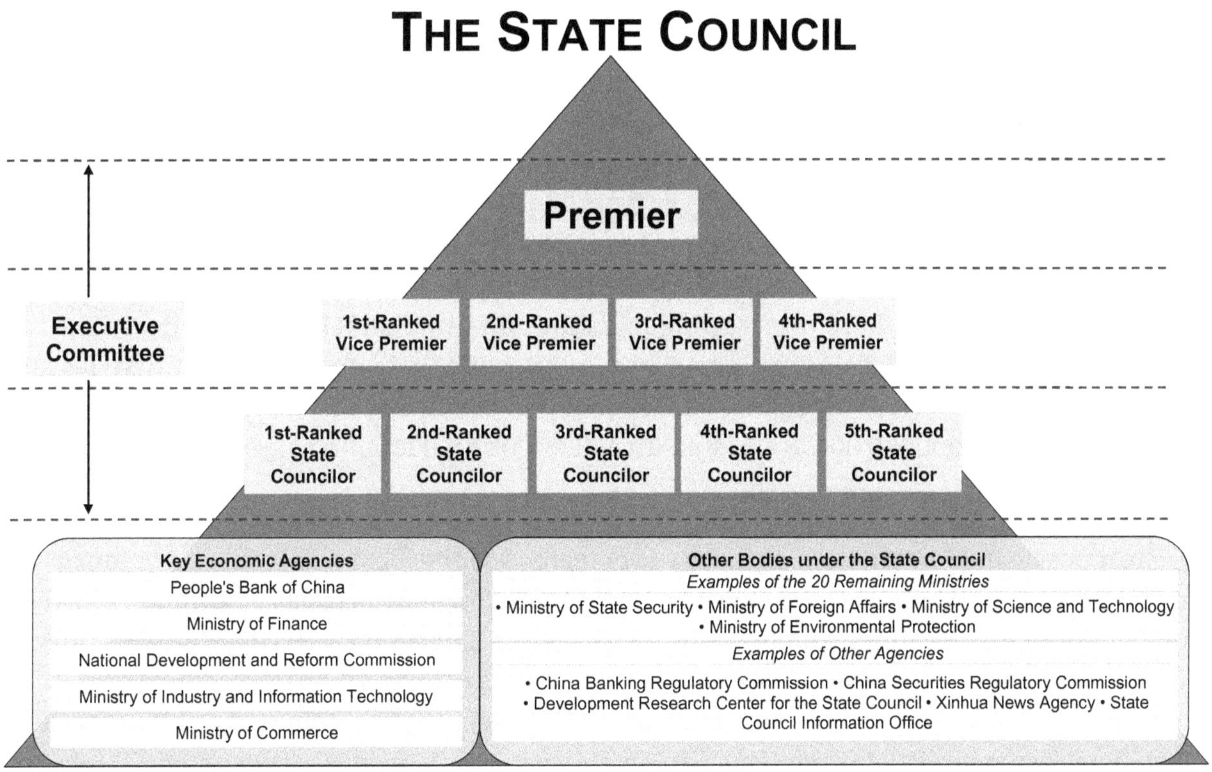


level bodies.[14] The executive committee meets weekly, and members rank above ordinary ministers. Their cross-cutting portfolios, particularly those of the vice premiers, allow them to play a key role in mediating disputes and coordinating policy among China's panoply of government agencies. Like all Chinese government and party agencies, the State Council has a general office, which plays a vital role in coordinating the flow of information and access to top leaders (though it is not a policymaking body).[15]

The full State Council meets only twice annually. Between these meetings, the executive committee is the primary decisionmaking body. Below the State Council executive, a wide array of committees and working groups bring together representatives from relevant ministries to coordinate on specific issues. There are also many ministerial- and vice-ministerial-level government agencies subordinate to (but not officially represented on) the State Council. These include influential official think tanks, policy research and legislative offices, news agencies, and other functional offices and commissions. Representatives from

14. A full list of government agencies represented on or subordinate to the State Council is available at http://english.gov.cn/state_council/2014/09/03/content_281474985533579.htm. While the roles of many agencies are in flux, among the most important ministerial-level bodies involved in the economic policymaking process and represented on the State Council are the National Development and Reform Commission (NDRC), the Ministry of Industry and Information Technology (MIIT), the Ministry of Finance (MOF), the Ministry of Commerce (MOFCOM), and the People's Bank of China (PBOC).

15. The current head of the State Council general office is State Councilor Yang Jing, who serves concurrently as the secretary-general of the State Council and secretary of the CCP Secretariat (its party equivalent).

these bodies sometimes attend plenary meetings, but only when invited and generally in a nonvoting capacity.[16]

Government agencies also wield significant influence in their own right. They (and their affiliated institutions) play major roles in conducting research, making policy recommendations, interpreting policy directives from higher levels of government, and promulgating regulations. Disagreements between ministries often create gridlock due to a combination of factors: equally ranked agencies cannot issue binding orders to one another; many ministries share overlapping mandates on functional issues; and decision-making at the ministry level is consensus based.[17] Despite their importance, ministries at the central level are relatively lightly staffed: out of more than 40 million civil servants nationwide, only about 60,000 are posted directly to ministries and commissions in Beijing.[18]

Most policy implementation authority is delegated to the local level. There are four formal levels of administration below the center[19]; in descending order of authority: provincial, prefectural, county, and township.[20] There are 31 provinces,[21] roughly 300 prefectures, nearly 3,000 counties, and over 40,000 townships.[22] Even where the central government in Beijing sets the rules, such as those governing taxation and public service provision, responsibility for implementing policy often falls to local governments. Units at the provincial level and below accounted for over 80 percent of official budgetary expendi-

16. Many of these institutions, while formally organized under the State Council, receive primary oversight from a separate party institution. For example, Xinhua News Agency is technically a ministry-level organization under the supervision of the State Council, but is in fact more closely overseen by the Central Committee Propaganda Office.

17. For example, the Ministry of Environmental Protection (MEP) is nominally the lead agency on environmental issues (along with the NDRC), yet it has historically had little power to enforce its mandate. Not only is it competing with the interests of more growth-focused ministries and provincial leaders, but management of critical issues, such as water pollution or heavy metal contamination of China's farmland, falls within the portfolios of other independent functional ministries, in this case the Ministry of Water Resources and Ministry of Agriculture, respectively. Meanwhile, local branches of the MEP, known as environmental protection bureaus, receive technical guidance from the MEP, but are funded and have their leadership appointed by local governments. For a more thorough treatment of this and other environmental issues, see Judith Shapiro, *China's Environmental Challenges* (Cambridge, UK: Polity Press, 2012).

18. According to Christine Wong, China has roughly 41 million public employees, excluding the armed forces and state-owned enterprises, while most central ministries have fewer than 1,000 each. Christine Wong, *Toward Building Performance-Oriented Management in China: The Critical Role of Monitoring and Evaluation and the Long Road Ahead*, ECD Working Papers No. 27 (Washington, DC: Independent Evaluation Group, World Bank, September 2012), http://siteresources.worldbank.org/EXTEVACAPDEV/Resources/wp_27_china_me.pdf.

19. The prefectural level is in fact not mentioned in China's state constitution, and some have argued it should be abolished to streamline interactions between levels of government.

20. Subprovincial, subprefectural, and sub-country-level units also exist, providing an additional level of complexity. For example, while both enjoy broadly comparable rights and responsibilities, a subprovincial-level city outranks a prefectural unit.

21. This is a slight oversimplification. Officially, there are 34 province-level administrative divisions in China. One of these is Taiwan, which China claims but does not administer. Two are the special administrative regions of Hong Kong and Macau, which enjoy a greater degree of autonomy than the 31 main Chinese provinces. Within these 31, 22 are provinces, 4 are province-level municipalities (Beijing, Tianjin, Shanghai, and Chongqing), and 5 are categorized as autonomous regions, due to the greater proportion of ethnic minority inhabitants.

22. For scale, an average county has half a million inhabitants. An average province has around 40 million.

tures in 2009, and for the vast majority of spending in areas such as education and environmental protection.[23] This makes their cooperation essential to achieving central objectives.

Local governments can also be important agents in the policymaking process; they compete for resources and attention from top-level leaders, for example, by conducting independent policy experiments or seeking support and funding for experimentation from higher administrative levels. Their superior local knowledge and de facto control over local branches of central-level ministries, such as the Ministry of Land and Resources, also means they have the capacity to subvert or covertly resist Beijing's policy objectives.[24]

# Operational Consequences

Throughout the post-Mao period, resources and authority have been divided between central and local government, with bargaining taking place vertically (within institutions) and horizontally (among them) to determine policy outcomes.[25] Rank within the Communist Party has been the main factor determining hierarchy within these relationships, creating a more expansive policy space than indicated solely by the structure of the Chinese state.[26] This complex policymaking space expanded during the Hu-Wen era to include a broad array of new or revitalized political actors, including activists, the media, and SOEs. At the same time, there remained a strong emphasis on consensus-based decisionmaking that prevailed since the immediate post-Mao period. The result was a pluralized system where the state maintained a major presence in the economy, but functional hierarchies were opaque, authority was fragmented, and policymaking was slowed by the need to seek consensus at a variety of levels and from a wide variety of gatekeepers.

By the end of the Hu-Wen administration, these developments and the increasing range of actors with influence on policy had reinforced fragmentation of decisionmaking and raised new barriers to policy implementation. Operationally, this meant that policies entailing substantive change from the status quo required sustained support and attention from officials at the highest levels in order to bypass cross-institutional disputes and ensure faithful implementation. Alongside the continued need for consensus across factions within the party, the consequence was an extremely laborious policymaking process (despite giving the outward appearance of authoritarian decisiveness).

---

23. Xiao Wang and Richard Herd, "The System of Revenue Sharing and Fiscal Transfers in China," OECD Economics Department Working Papers, February 27, 2013, http://www.oecd.org/officialdocuments/publicdisplaydocumentpdf/?cote=ECO/WKP%282013%2922&docLanguage=En.

24. The exact reporting relationship between central government ministries and their local counterparts varies with the agency. For example, the NDRC directly supervises branches in all 31 provinces; MOFCOM functions are handled by both directly managed officials and locally managed commerce commissions at the provincial level; and, as discussed above, the MEP provides technical guidance to local environmental protection bureaus, but their funding and appointments are controlled by local officials.

25. Kenneth G. Lieberthal and David M. Lampton, eds., *Bureaucracy, Politics, and Decision Making in Post-Mao China* (Berkeley: University of California Press, 1992).

26. Susan V. Lawrence and Michael F. Martin, "Understanding China's Political System," Congressional Research Service, March 20, 2013, https://www.fas.org/sgp/crs/row/R41007.pdf.

# Structural Changes under Xi Jinping

The Xi administration, and Xi Jinping himself, has acted to decisively reverse these trends. Where Hu and Wen left economic policymaking largely in the hands of the state and favored heavy state intervention in day-to-day economic affairs, Xi has sought to reemphasize the party's role in economic policymaking and withdraw the state from unnecessary activities.

Beginning in the lead-up to the Third Plenum, Xi Jinping relied on officials seconded from the CFELSG to draft what would become the Decision. The drafting committee was chaired by Xi Jinping and composed of other top leaders—including fellow PBSC members Liu Yunshan and Zhang Gaoli—and key experts. Meanwhile, the committee's day-to-day administration and work were overseen by Liu He,[27] a noted economist often referred to as "China's Larry Summers,"[28] who simultaneously serves as the director of the office of the CFELSG.

The Third Plenum then announced the creation of a new Comprehensively Deepening Reform Leading Small Group (CDRLSG), marking an enhanced role for LSGs in the economic policymaking process under Xi. Party documents have designated this body to play the central role in coordinating China's reforms through 2020, when its remit officially expires. Xi heads the body and three additional PBSC members serve as deputy chairs, giving it unrivaled authority as it seeks to implement reform.[29] The CDRLSG also has its own general office, or nerve center, led by Wang Huning, a Politburo member and head of the influential Central Committee Policy Research Office, where the staff for this office is located. Below the main LSG are six functional offices, each dedicated to managing a different aspect of reform, such as the economy and environment.[30]

The creation of this group demonstrated that Xi had the clout to create structural solutions at the highest levels of China's policymaking apparatus to get around the gridlock that had characterized the state machinery for much of the past decade. In a move unprecedented for an LSG, the group has even been replicated at all provincial and prefectural-level governments in China and in all ministries and government agencies. Each of these groups is headed by the most senior official in the relevant administrative jurisdiction.

---

27. Liu He also provides an example of the many hats worn by high-level Chinese leaders. He is a member of the CCP Central Committee, a minister-level vice director of the NDRC, a codirector of the office of the CDRLSG, and the director of the office of the CFELSG.

28. This moniker was first applied by Cheng Li, a specialist in China's leadership. Michael Forsythe and Dune Lawrence, "Liu He as China's Larry Summers Makes Politburo Appreciate U.S.," Bloomberg, September 24, 2009, http://www.bloomberg.com/apps/news?pid=newsarchive&sid=aKp9wybwC4HM.

29. The three are Li Keqiang, Liu Yunshan, and Zhang Gaoli. They are ranked 2nd, 5th, and 7th on the PBSC, respectively. For a list of their primary areas of responsibility, see Susan V. Lawrence, "China's Political Institutions and Leaders in Charts," Congressional Research Service, November 12, 2013, https://www.fas.org/sgp/crs/row/R43303.pdf.

30. The six groups are economy and ecology, democracy and justice, culture, society, party construction, and discipline and supervision. See Appendix I for details.

That the CDRLSG is a party body designated as the primary driver of reform, and that Xi is seeking to ensure implementation through party rather than official state channels, underscores his emphasis on the centrality of the CCP in both setting policy priorities and driving their implementation. Its creation may also have finally put to rest the enduring intraparty debate running throughout the reform era over the wisdom and efficacy of seeking to separate party and government functions.

The new LSG also provides a reminder of the nature of the challenges Xi and top leaders are seeking to overcome. As discussed earlier, despite the CCP's continued monopoly on political power, various actors compete intensely to influence policy. Powerful vested interests, such as giant SOEs, fight to insulate themselves from reform. Government agencies, such as the influential NDRC, are divided over reform, and many seek to protect the interests of those they regulate. Scholars, think tanks, and government research institutes compete to shape the ideas of top leaders. Provincial leaders lobby for projects and initiatives that will support local priorities. Even institutions once less influential in policymaking, such as traditional and social media, nongovernmental organizations, and civil society groups, are finding new opportunities to advance their agendas. All of this has contributed to making China's policymaking space increasingly messy, complicated, and, in a word, pluralistic.

# 4 Traditional Characteristics of Chinese Economic Policymaking

Although the shape of the Chinese economic policymaking apparatus has proven quite fluid during the period of "reform and opening," many characteristics of policymaking have remained consistent. These reflect the enduring realities of China's vast population and geography, its one-party political system, and the overarching goal that has guided successive generations of Chinese leaders: to achieve the great rejuvenation of the Chinese nation under the leadership of the Chinese Communist Party.

## Coordination Challenges

All large organizations, especially governments, face coordination challenges, but China's are particularly severe, despite (and in part because of) the top-down nature of the Chinese political system. This has improved as successive reform drives and the gradual retreat from direct state control over the economy have slimmed China's bureaucracy:[1] in 1981, there were exactly 100 government ministries; by 2013, that number had fallen to 25 (though the number of ministry-ranked agencies is much higher).[2] Nonetheless, serious coordination problems remain.

One factor is the frequent jurisdictional overlap between government ministries. This is in part deliberate. Lacking any formal system of checks and balances, the fragmentation of authority and information across functional agencies serves the political purpose of helping to avoid concentrations of power growing up outside of Zhongnanhai.[3] On the other hand, it is an impediment to coherent policymaking. Combined with a strong emphasis on consensus-based policymaking, fragmentation makes cooperation essential to developing and implementing policy shifts. However, because ministries often face competing

1. This restructuring took place over repeated cycles of contraction and expansion. For example, the 100 organizations of 1981 were downsized to 61 in 1982, but had expanded to 72 by 1987. For more, see the chapter "Bureaucracy and Governance," in Yongnian Zheng, *Contemporary China: A History since 1978* (Malden, MA: Wiley-Blackwell, 2013).

2. For example, the heads of China's three financial regulatory commissions are ministry-ranked, as are the heads of Xinhua News, the Chinese Academy of Social Sciences, and the Development Research Center of the State Council, but none are represented on the State Council.

3. Zhongnanhai is the Chinese equivalent of the White House, a leadership compound located in central Beijing that houses the main offices of both the State Council and the Communist Party.

## Anti-Monopoly Law (AML) Enforcement Structure

An illustration of China's coordination challenges

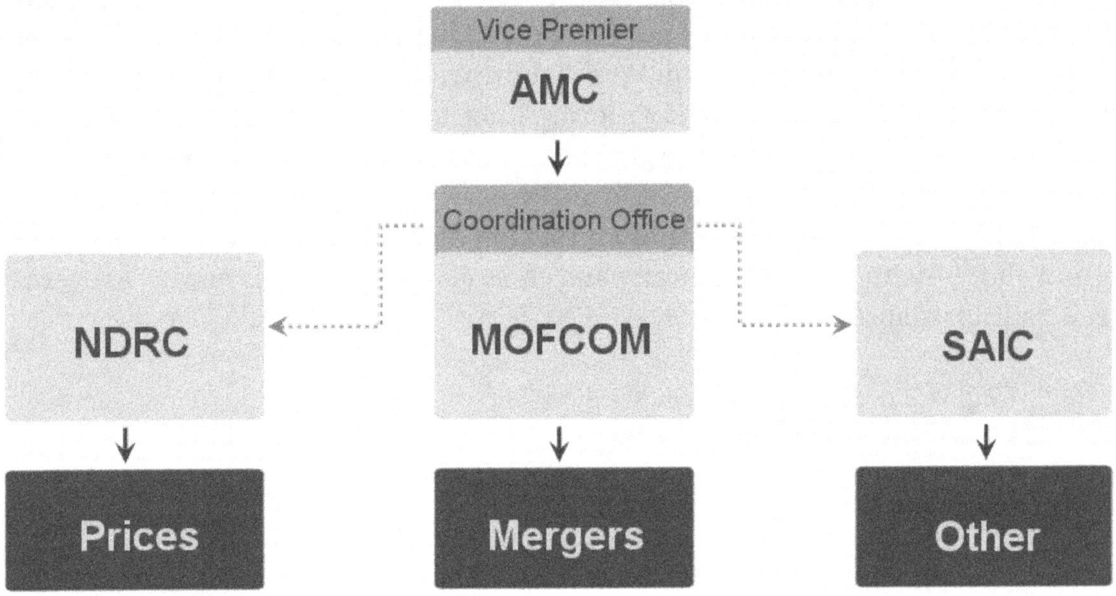


The structure for enforcing China's 2010 AML helps to illustrate China's coordination challenges. AML enforcement is technically overseen by the Anti-Monopoly Commission (AMC), an 18-member interministerial body directly under the State Council. It is chaired by a vice premier (previously Wang Qishan, currently Wang Yang). The agency responsible for hosting the AMC office is the Ministry of Commerce (MOFCOM), which is supposed to coordinate day-to-day AML enforcement on behalf of the AMC; in fact, each of the three ministry-level agencies responsible for AML implementation often acts autonomously. The NDRC oversees price-related rules, MOFCOM oversees mergers, and the State Administration of Industry and Commerce (SAIC) handles non-price-related rules, such as abuse of market dominance.

objectives and cannot issue binding orders to bodies of equal formal rank (i.e., other ministries), gridlock and stovepiping are common. Other aspects of Chinese politics further exacerbate this challenge: high-ranking officials must compete with each other for future promotions and to gain the favor of top leaders, which often reduces the incentive to compromise.

Another issue behind China's poor coordination is its approach. When addressing issues that range across functional mandates, representatives of all relevant agencies (and others that deem the issue within their "turf") become part of an ad hoc committee. Either after extensive negotiation or based on a mandate from above, one agency is then designated as the lead and placed in charge of coordinating on the project. This usually results in the establishment of a specialized coordinating office within that ministry. But in the highly rank-conscious environment of Chinese public administration, the effectiveness of coordination is then almost completely dependent on the lead ministry's influence within the broader policymaking apparatus—or its ability to attract and retain the attention of top leaders.[4]

Efforts to solve this problem through institutional redesigns—such as the creation of "super ministries" with broad portfolios and explicit mandates to oversee coordination—had little positive effect during the Hu-Wen administration. The NDRC is the most obvious example of this: rather than improving coordination, its role as a "mini–State Council" became a major contributing factor to gridlock and helped concentrate and empower vested interests opposed to structural reform. Instead, most examples of effective coordination are the result of sustained attention from top leaders—typically at the vice-premier level and above—with both the authority and cross-cutting portfolios needed to overcome bureaucratic resistance.

## Center-Local Relations

There is a Chinese saying that "the mountains are high and the emperor far away." This reflects China's history of decentralized government and the modern reality that much policy is made outside Beijing. This is clearest when looking at trends in public spending. Reforms in 1994 aggressively recentralized tax revenues. However, since the mid-2000s, spending at the provincial level and below has regularly accounted for more than 75 percent of total government expenditure and the vast majority of spending on public services, such as health care, education, and social welfare.[5]

The center-local divide is even more important than the fiscal situation suggests. Since the early stages of reform, local leaders at all levels have been evaluated for promotion according to their ability to meet targets set by the immediately superior level of government.[6] The precise metrics used for performance assessment have evolved with time, but two targets have consistently remained top priorities: economic growth and social stability. This system carried distinct advantages in the early stages of China's development, spurring intense competition among local leaders to generate growth-boosting policy

4. Even a powerful ministry does not guarantee a speedy or coherent process of policy generation. For example, the NDRC, long regarded as China's single most powerful government bureaucracy, was the lead agency in charge of developing China's urbanization plan jointly with over a dozen additional ministries. But the plan, released in March 2014, nonetheless suffered multiple delays and arrived a year later than initially promised.

5. These "unfunded mandates" have been a major factor behind the rapid buildup of local government debt and the growth of local government financing vehicles. While the central government does transfer a significant portion of fiscal revenues to the provinces, the process for deciding the size of transfers is opaque, largely subjective, and not directly tied to expenditure responsibilities. See Christine Wong, *Toward Building Performance-Oriented Management in China: The Critical Role of Monitoring and Evaluation and the Long Road Ahead*, ECD Working Papers No. 27 (Washington, DC: Independent Evaluation Group, World Bank, September 2012), http://siteresources.worldbank.org/EXTEVACAPDEV/Resources/wp_27_china_me.pdf.

6. This so-called one-level-down management system entails the appointee at each administrative level being appointed and managed by the post at the next higher level. Under this system, promotion decisions and supervision are dependent on immediate superiors rather than central authorities. See Wang Xiaoqi, *China's Civil Service Reform* (London: Routledge, 2013).

innovations in their jurisdictions, the most successful of which provided templates for pilot policies elsewhere. Even when tasked with conflicting objectives, such as environmental protection, local officials' incentives were clear. In addition to being a hard target and easily measurable, growth had the advantage of indirectly promoting social stability, enabling greater expenditure on public works, and providing officials with opportunities for personal enrichment.

But as Beijing has sought to balance a growing array of national policy priorities, such as improved social welfare and clean government, and to impose more "top-level design," the downsides of decentralization have also become clear. Inconsistent standards and regulations across internal borders complicate the operating environment for businesses. Detailed local knowledge, which allows provincial leaders to interpret Beijing's often vague policy pronouncements to suit conditions on the ground, have turned from advantage to obstacle as national leaders' objectives have come into conflict with local priorities. Difficulties in addressing widespread air pollution are an example of this: while the pollution itself is widespread, the costs of addressing it in terms of reduced growth, lower revenues, and higher unemployment are borne locally. This makes the decision to impose antipollution measures highly political, requiring costly efforts (and compensation) to avoid instability and create incentives for compliance.

Much of the responsibility for these problems also falls on Beijing. In attempting to bridge the central-local divide and establish specific metrics for how to govern 1.36 billion people, national leaders have often created incentives for their subordinates to meet measurable targets at the expense of policy outcomes, or to create new problems by blindly pursuing unrealistic targets. For example, central mandates for local governments to improve health care coverage and to increase spending on public education and infrastructure—unaccompanied by any new formal sources of revenue—were major factors behind the worrisome growth in local debt over recent years.[7] Despite Beijing's promises that it has moved away from "GDP-obsessed" assessments and embraced a wider set of priorities, the continued posting of an annual growth target—even one that central leaders have stressed in recent years is nonbinding[8]—underscores that Chinese leaders will face significant challenges in creating the right mix of incentives to implement more balanced policies.

## Experimentation

Experimentation has been a hallmark of Chinese leaders' approach to advancing reform ever since Deng Xiaoping's famous decision in 1980 to open the Shenzhen Special Economic

7. Another was the growth targets themselves, which incentivized local leaders to generate revenues from land sales and other extrabudgetary financing that could then be funneled into GDP-boosting investments.

8. For an optimistic view of the changing nature of Chinese targets, see Stephen Roach, "The End of Chinese Central Planning," *Project Syndicate*, March 27, 2014, http://www.project-syndicate.org/commentary/stephen-s--roach-reports-that-the-country-s-top-economic-officials-have-all-but-abandoned-traditional-growth-targets.

Zone and allow foreign direct investment into China. Experiments advanced from Beijing limit the political and economic risk of testing new policies. If these pilots prove successful, they provide evidence for those interested in implementing reform more broadly. Further pilots can then be tested in new areas, and the most successful approaches expanded nationwide. If an experiment fails, the failure is localized and cannot independently generate a large-scale threat to economic or social stability. This practice of experimentation is in keeping with the halting, risk-averse approach that has been typical of the Chinese economic reform process and is in keeping with Beijing's strong emphasis on maintaining social stability.

Ambitious local officials interested in improving their chances at promotion can also generate experiments independently. Top-level Chinese documents, such as the Third Plenum Decision, are typically rife with vague, confusing, and often contradictory language, with the specifics then left to the functional agencies and lower levels of government to define and implement. At its best, this ambiguity allows ambitious local leaders to produce innovative policies based on knowledge of ground-level conditions, which then attract the attention of higher-level policymakers, who can scale up and implement these reforms on a broader basis. Local leaders might also secure tacit support from higher-level leaders to pilot pet projects, the success of which can advance the aforementioned leaders' agenda (while providing plausible deniability in case of failure). This system has long been vital to China's ability to achieve reforms despite its overall top-down political system.

Experimentation also carries risks. The decision to launch the Shanghai Free-Trade Zone (FTZ) in September 2013 (discussed in more detail in Chapter 5) as a trial for capital market reforms and new models of administration indicates that Chinese leaders are still most comfortable advancing reform through contained experiments. But there is some question of whether or not this approach of "crossing the river while feeling the stones" will work as reforms enter deeper water—and whether this preference for experimentation could become an excuse to avoid embracing bolder reforms. For example, the development of service industries that is at the heart of the Shanghai experiment is qualitatively different from the manufacturing-sector development that took place in Shenzhen. There is a distinct possibility that trying to isolate these industries and reforms from impacting the broader economy will undermine the increased service-sector competitiveness that Beijing seeks to encourage.

# External Pressure

Despite the primacy of domestic drivers in Chinese policymaking, external pressure exerts an important influence on the incentives facing China's leaders. At the central government level, it can provide leverage and an organizing principle for leaders taking on domestic opposition. As discussed earlier, former premier Zhu Rongji famously used the process of negotiating China's accession to the WTO as a club to beat back vested interests, downsizing a bloated state-owned sector to lay the groundwork for a decade of phenomenal growth. At the local level, competition for foreign direct investment (FDI) has had an important impact in shaping leaders' incentives. Officials seeking to boost growth, generate employment, and move into higher value-added production areas have strong incentives to compete for foreign direct investment, particularly in technology-intensive sectors.

At the same time, China's subsequent foot-dragging on implementing its WTO commitments and frequent examples of outright or circumspect noncompliance illustrate the limits of external pressure to produce change.[9] Chinese leaders use external pressure as a pragmatic tool for advancing their specific interests. Their commitment to general principles, such as free trade, remains selective and narrow.[10] Thus, it is important to distinguish Beijing's use of external pressure as a tool to drive its own reform agenda and the effectiveness of external pressure in shaping Chinese domestic economic policy—particularly given the views of the Chinese leadership on economic development as central to China's "comprehensive security."

Today, growing momentum in international negotiations, such as those to establish a Trans-Pacific Partnership (TPP) and a U.S.-China Bilateral Investment Treaty (BIT), are creating changes in China's external environment that may be playing a similar role to the WTO accession process in encouraging Chinese leaders to advance new pilots, such as the Shanghai FTZ. However, it is uncertain whether these will have a comparable transformative impact. Moreover, as the Xi administration considers how to pursue reforms in the context of new external pressures, it also faces new challenges. Not only is the Chinese economy far larger than it was in Deng or Zhu's time, but it is much more deeply intertwined with the global economy than in the past. Thus, for example, the effort to liberalize and open China's capital markets is complicated by the risk of rapid capital inflows and/or outflows in a globalized financial system.

---

9. The Office of the U.S. Trade Representative (USTR) prepares an annual report to Congress on China's WTO compliance, which remain extensive. See USTR, *2014 Report to Congress on China's WTO Compliance* (Washington, DC: USTR, December 2014), https://ustr.gov/sites/default/files/2014-Report-to-Congress-Final.pdf.

10. Robert Sutter, "China's Grand Strategy in Asia" (testimony before the U.S.-China Economic and Security Review Commission, March 13, 2014), http://www.uscc.gov/sites/default/files/SUTTER_Testimony.pdf.

# 5 Decisionmaking in the Financial Sector

## Introduction

Financial reform is central to rebalancing the Chinese economy toward a new model of consumption-led growth. Since the global financial crisis, China's financial system has generated an estimated $6.8 trillion in "wasted investment," at the same time that GDP and productivity growth have dramatically slowed.[1] China's current leaders have accordingly identified financial reform as a priority in their overall economic reform agenda, released in November 2013. This agenda promises reform in the three primary areas where significant controls still prevent the market from playing a "decisive role" in capital allocation: interest rates, the exchange rate, and the capital account.

If implemented, these reforms have the potential to not only transform China's financial system but also help unlock the new sources of growth required for China to become a "modern, harmonious, and creative high-income society."[2] At the same time, efforts to remove existing controls and build a modern financial system also highlight the challenges facing China's reformers, and provide a window into Chinese economic policymaking under the Xi Jinping administration. Against a backdrop of slowing growth and rising debt, the reforms are risky and technically complex and face opposition from a host of powerful vested interests. This makes the strategy and process of reform implementation as important as the substance of the reforms themselves, and allows financial reform to serve as a lens for understanding the process of economic policymaking under the Xi Jinping administration.

This study focuses on financial reform for three primary reasons. First, financial reform is an area where success or failure has clear implications for the health of the overall economy. Second, Beijing has signaled that financial reform is a priority area within its own overall economic agenda. This makes it a useful test of the leadership's credibility—both its ability to deliver on its reform agenda and its willingness to give

1. Jamil Anderlini, "China has 'wasted' $6.8tn in investment, warn Beijing researchers," *Financial Times*, November 27, 2014, www.ft.com/intl/cms/s/0/002a1978-7629-11e4-9761-00144feabdc0.html.

2. This is the original title of a 2012 report coauthored by The World Bank and the Development Research Center of the State Council, a Chinese government think tank. The report was later released with the words "high-income" removed from the title. See World Bank and Development Research Center of the State Council, People's Republic of China, *China 2030: Building a Modern, Harmonious, and Creative Society* (Washington, DC: World Bank, 2013), http://www.worldbank.org/content/dam/Worldbank/document/China-2030-complete.pdf.

markets the promised "decisive role." Third, finance is an area where policymaking is comparatively centralized and the number of bureaucratic players relatively small. This gives Zhongnanhai important advantages in implementing financial reform according to "top-level design." Progress (or the lack thereof) on financial reform can thus, to a certain extent, provide a barometer for how Beijing is faring with its overall reform agenda.

## FINANCIAL REFORM AND CHINA'S ECONOMIC REBALANCING

The structure of the Chinese financial system is a major factor behind the country's macroeconomic imbalances. Controls over key prices, most notably bank deposit rates, systematically subsidize investment at the cost of consumption. In recent years, this "financial repression" has caused investment as a share of GDP to regularly approach 50 percent, contributed to sustained current account surpluses, and helped to push China's debt-to-GDP ratio above 250 percent.[3] The tendency of Chinese banks, which still supply the majority of credit, to favor larger borrowers in the industrial sector has further exacerbated this issue. Instead of supporting the growth of small and medium-sized enterprises (SMEs) in the services sector,[4] where employment and productivity gains are greatest, banks have concentrated on lending to well-connected industrial concerns in overcapacity sectors.[5]

This has left financing gaps that a large "shadow banking" sector has developed to fill. Shadow banking includes all forms of nonbank credit intermediation—both licit and illicit—as well as nontraditional lending activities by banks (often conducted on an off-balance-sheet basis). Examples of these activities include "trust loans, company-to-company entrusted loans, corporate bonds, and bankers' acceptances."[6] These nontraditional lending activities fill unmet demand for credit and, to an extent, encourage more market-based pricing of risk.[7] They have also contributed to China's rapid debt build-up and magnified the overall level of risk and opacity in the domestic financial system.

The remaining controls on China's financial system are relatively few in number but have been large in impact. The first is a deposit-rate ceiling set by the PBOC. China lacks strong social welfare protections, and channels for individuals to invest their savings are limited. In this context, by imposing a cap on the interest rate banks can pay depositors,

---

3. Pedro Nicolaci da Costa, "China's Total Debt Load Equals 282% of GDP, Raising Economic Risks," *Wall Street Journal*, February 4, 2015, http://blogs.wsj.com/economics/2015/02/04/chinas-total-debt-load-equals-282-of-gdp-raising-its-economic-risks/.

4. Financing for SMEs is a problem many countries face. In international comparison, the Chinese financial system performs fairly well in providing SMEs with *access* to financing, though the *cost* of that financing is often prohibitive. For a more detailed discussion of this evolving issue, see Nicholas Borst, "Does China have an SME Lending Problem?" *China Economic Watch*, August 22, 2014, http://blogs.piie.com/china/?p=4025.

5. There has been some improvement on this issue in recent years, which is discussed in considerably more detail by Nicholas Lardy in his most recent book. See Nicholas R. Lardy, *Markets over Mao: The Rise of Private Business in China* (Washington, DC: Peterson Institute for International Economics, 2014).

6. Nicholas Borst, "Flying Blind," *International Economy* (Winter 2014), http://www.international-economy.com/TIE_W14_Borst.pdf.

7. Chi Lo, "China's Systemic Risk: Shadow Banking," BNP Paribas, June 2014, http://institutional.bnpparibas-ip.com/chinas-systemic-risk-shadow-banking/.

the Chinese authorities force households to accept a below-market rate of return on their savings, encouraging oversaving and underconsumption—or the seeking of higher rates of return via risky wealth management products.[8] For banks and their borrowers, the deposit rate ceiling acts as a subsidy, artificially lowering their funding costs and contributing to overinvestment in capital-intensive industries.[9]

Complementing this policy is China's closed capital account.[10] Despite significant moves to liberalize China's direct investment regime, opportunities for both inbound and outbound portfolio investment remain limited. This restricts the ability of savers to move their funds abroad in search of a higher return, dampening their ability to consume and confining them to the limited pool of assets available domestically (such as real estate and, increasingly, wealth management products). A third pillar of this system is China's managed exchange rate regime, the maintenance of which has led to the accumulation of over $3.5 trillion in official reserves.[11] An undervalued RMB has historically helped to fuel exports and make imports artificially expensive in the Chinese market, protecting domestic industry at the cost of suppressed household consumption.

## FINANCIAL REFORM IN THE THIRD PLENUM AGENDA

Financial reform features prominently within the Third Plenum Decision and is a key element of the overall strategy to give the market a "decisive role" in resource allocation. Section 12 of the document presents a sweeping array of market-based reforms. These include liberalization of interest rates, the exchange rate, and the capital account, precisely the reforms needed to address the aforementioned imbalances. Section 12 also describes the institutional reforms needed to support this liberalization and greater marketization of the Chinese financial system. These include the introduction of a deposit insurance scheme, strengthened and better-coordinated regulatory supervision, and the development

8. The reasons underpinning China's high household savings rates are much debated, and deposit rate controls are not the only factor. For example, Liu (2014) estimates that job uncertainty resulting from market-based reforms accounted for about a third of Chinese urban household wealth accumulation from 1995 to 2002. Another key factor is China's relatively threadbare social safety net. For more, see Zheng Liu, "Job Uncertainty and Chinese Household Savings," Federal Reserve Bank of San Francisco, February 3, 2014, http://www.frbsf.org/economic-research/publications/economic-letter/2014/february/job-uncertainty-china-household-savings-state-owned-enterprises-iron-rice-bowl/.

9. The effect of the deposit ceiling as a subsidy has been reduced in recent years, as a host of new vehicles for savings has emerged to compete with banks for deposits, such as wealth management products and Internet finance. Many of these benefit from an implicit guarantee that the local or central government will step in to prevent default, though the expected introduction of a new deposit insurance system designed to make explicit what products are and are not guaranteed will likely impact this dynamic.

10. For a review of China's capital account restrictions as of October 2014, see IMF, *Annual Report on Exchange Arrangements and Exchange Restrictions 2014* (Washington, DC: IMF, October 2014), https://www.imf.org/external/pubs/nft/2014/areaers/ar2014.pdf.

11. The extent of China's RMB undervaluation is much debated. For example, Subramanian and Kessler (2014) use a purchasing-power-parity-based methodology to argue that the RMB is fairly valued. In its 2014 Article IV review for China, the IMF assessed that the RMB remained "moderately undervalued" as of July 2014. However, in the first months of 2015, the RMB has instead faced pressure to depreciate. Martin Kessler and Arvind Subramanian, "Is the Renminbi Still Undervalued? Not According to New PPP Estimates," *RealTime Economic Issues Watch,* May 1, 2014, http://blogs.piie.com/realtime/?p=4300; IMF, *People's Republic of China: 2014 Article IV Consultation* (Washington, DC: IMF, July 2014), https://www.imf.org/external/pubs/ft/scr/2014/cr14235.pdf.

of more direct financing methods. Financial reform is also identified throughout the Decision as key to solving other problems, such as improving the allocation of funds to support technological advancement.[12]

Since the Third Plenum, a host of high-profile Chinese financial policymakers—and People's Bank of China Governor Zhou Xiaochuan in particular—has further clarified the direction of reform. In December 2013, Governor Zhou presented a roadmap for financial reform, promising to "speed up" reforms in all three of the aforementioned areas.[13] In a speech the following March and again in July 2014, he went even further, suggesting that bank deposit rates could be liberalized "within about two years." These statements from the PBOC have been echoed by the leadership of other key regulatory agencies, including the China Banking Regulatory Commission (CBRC). In an October 2014 article published in the leading Communist Party journal *Seeking Truth*, CBRC Chairman Shang Fulin stressed the need to use market-based reforms of interest rates and greater financial innovation to improve the efficiency of capital allocation, while improving financial regulation to ensure stability.[14] Along with repeated mentions by President Xi and Premier Li, these statements indicate the high priority that Chinese leaders are placing on financial reform.

## FINANCIAL REFORM AND ECONOMIC POLICYMAKING

Three factors make financial reform a useful lens for understanding the characteristics of Chinese economic policymaking under Xi, as well as the challenges of overall economic reform.

First, financial reform is an area where success or failure has clear implications for the health of the overall economy. Should China fail to build a financial system capable of efficiently allocating credit to a modern market economy, the imbalances described above could deepen rather than correct. The country will likely struggle in its transition to a new consumption-led growth model as inefficient capital allocation harms productivity growth (particularly in the services sector), leading the overall macro environment to deteriorate, and raising the risk that unproductive debts will further mount and eventually produce a crisis. While carrying its own set of risks—among them, a weakening of the party's direct influence over economic outcomes—transitioning to a competitive, market-based financial system capable of promoting free entry and exit of firms and efficient allocation of credit is almost universally regarded as essential to China's continued economic development. Market-based financial reforms would not only provide a boost to growth but also generate

12. For a comprehensive review of the Third Plenum Decision, see Daniel H. Rosen, *Avoiding the Blind Alley: China's Economic Overhaul and Its Global Implications* (New York: Asia Society Policy Institute, October 2014), http://asiasociety.org/files/pdf/AvoidingtheBlindAlley_FullReport.pdf.

13. Zhou Xiaochuan, "Road map for financial reform," *China Daily*, December 11, 2013, http://usa.chinadaily.com.cn/opinion/2013-12/11/content_17166127.htm; Zhou Xiaochuan, "Road map for financial reform," *China Daily*, December 28, 2013, http://usa.chinadaily.com.cn/opinion/2013-12/11/content_17166127.htm.

14. Shang Fulin, "Finding the Right Balance between Financial Innovation and Stability," *Qiushi* 6, no. 4 (October 2014), http://english.qstheory.cn/2014-11/15/c_1113078071.htm.

strong pressures for reform in other areas and help to rebalance the Chinese economy toward a more sustainable growth model.

Second, Beijing has signaled that financial reform is a priority area within its own overall economic agenda. This makes it a useful test of the leadership's credibility—particularly its willingness to give markets the promised "decisive role." Beijing has long sought to exercise strict control over finance as a core part of not only its development strategy but also its efforts to maintain the Communist Party's "leading role" in the domestic political system.[15] How leaders proceed with financial reform implementation can provide indication of how they will attempt to balance this "leading role" for the party with the "decisive role" accorded the market. Given the array of vested interests that benefit from the current financial system, such as local governments and SOEs, financial reform will also be a key test of political will.

Third, finance is a good testing ground for the ability of the current leadership in Beijing to manage the overall reform process at a difficult time of transition—the focus of this study. Contrary to other aspects of the reform agenda, such as urbanization, Beijing has direct influence over all of the main levers of financial policy, from interest rates to the payments system. This gives Chinese leaders and central technocrats a strong hand in shaping the reform process—and therefore less excuse for failure. At the same time, financial reform will test some of the enduring characteristics of Chinese policymaking described in Chapter 4. For example, experimentation may not be a viable approach in a porous sector like financial services where both innovation and risk can spread rapidly. Similarly, external forces both facilitate and complicate financial reform, as pressure builds up for capital to flow both in and out of the country. And it remains to be seen whether Beijing's policymakers can pull off the proper sequencing of interest-rate deregulation and capital-account liberalization while avoiding financial instability, against the backdrop of an opaque and fast-evolving set of risks.

The remainder of this chapter is divided into four sections. The first provides background on the development of China's financial system over the past 35 years. The next describes the structure of the financial policymaking apparatus. This is followed by three case studies covering interest rate, exchange rate, and capital account reform. A final section reviews characteristics of policymaking illustrated by these case studies and assesses their implications for financial reform moving forward.

## The Evolution of China's Financial System

Since the start of "reform and opening," the evolution of the Chinese financial system has mirrored the transformation of the economy. In 1978, the PBOC managed over 90 percent of China's financial assets, acting as both a central and commercial bank. Central planners

15. Carl Walter and Fraser Howie, *Red Capitalism: The Fragile Financial Foundation of China's Extraordinary Rise* (Hoboken, NJ: Wiley, 2012); Victor C. Shih, *Factions and Finance in China: Elite Conflict and Inflation* (Cambridge, UK: Cambridge University Press, 2009).

determined the allocation of real and financial resources, rather than expected rates of return. Today, the Chinese financial system is far more diverse and, like the economy as a whole, far more market-oriented. New financial intermediaries and nontraditional lending platforms, such as Internet finance vehicles, have proliferated alongside state-owned megabanks and traditional commercial lenders. The size of the financial system relative to the overall economy has swelled from 32 percent of GDP in 1978 to over 250 percent today.

As this system has grown in size and complexity, China has built a sophisticated financial regulatory apparatus charged with its oversight. In many respects, this apparatus closely resembles that of many Western economies: it features a modern central bank, responsible for managing overall credit conditions and maintaining financial stability, as well as specialized regulatory institutions, such as the CBRC and China Insurance Regulatory Commission (CIRC). If the financial reforms outlined in the Third Plenum Decision are implemented, these similarities will continue to deepen over time, as Beijing introduces new institutions, such as a planned deposit insurance facility, that are standard features of a modern financial system.

However, the resemblance between the Chinese and Western financial systems can be overstated. The evolution of China's financial system reflects its dual mandate: to allocate capital in a manner that promotes stable growth and the modernization of the Chinese economy; and to serve as a tool for maintaining the power and control of the Communist Party. This has meant both a gradual introduction of market discipline in the financial system and the maintenance of a high degree of political control over market participants. This closeness of finance and politics in China is evidenced both by the formal structure of the system, which is dominated by large state-owned banks with government-appointed leadership, and by the close informal ties that exist between financial institutions and governments at the central and local levels.[16]

The Third Plenum reforms promise to reshape this relationship, minimizing political interference in everyday decisions where market-determined outcomes more effectively serve party objectives. However, in the minds of Chinese leaders, giving the market a decisive role in capital allocation does not mean eliminating public ownership and control. The stated goal of the reforms is to produce a stable and efficient financial system capable of supporting a new, more sustainable, consumption-led growth model. Or, to borrow a phrase from a 2009 document released by the State Council, to create a financial system "commensurate with [China's] economic strength."[17] History suggests this implies a reduc-

---

16. For a concise overview of the Chinese financial system in the context of Western financial systems, see Douglas J. Elliott and Kai Yan, *The Chinese Financial System: An Introduction and Overview*, John L. Thornton China Center Monograph Series, No. 6 (Washington, DC: Brookings, July 2013), http://www.brookings.edu/~/media/research/files/papers/2013/07/01%20chinese%20financial%20system%20elliott%20yan/chinese%20financial%20system%20elliott%20yan.pdf.

17. The State Council, "Opinions on Accelerating Shanghai's Developing Its Modern Service and Advanced Manufacturing Industries, and Its Development into an International Financial Center and an International Shipping Center," endorsed by an executive meeting of the State Council on March 25, 2009. Quoted in Patrick Hess, "China's Financial System: Past Reforms, Future Ambitions, and Current State," *Currency Cooperation in East Asia*, ed. Frank Rövekamp and Hanns Günther (New York: Springer, 2014).

tion in direct state ownership and control over the financial system and greater international openness, but only to the extent and in a manner that serves Chinese leaders' enduring political goals: maintaining stability and achieving the "great rejuvenation of the Chinese nation."[18]

## THE EARLY REFORM PERIOD: 1978–1992

At the start of "reform and opening" in 1978, the sophistication of China's financial system reflected both the country's overall low level of development and the ancillary role of finance in a planned economy.[19] As previously mentioned, the PBOC managed upwards of 90 percent of the country's financial assets, serving as both China's central and sole commercial bank under the control of the Ministry of Finance (MOF). Central planners determined the allocation of resources, rather than financial considerations, and investment was financed through government budgets. Domestic stock, bond, and insurance markets were nonexistent, and all foreign currency was controlled by the central government, which distributed it at an officially determined rate of exchange. Only 15 years later, banks had become the dominant source of financing in the Chinese economy, Beijing was on the verge of ending a cumbersome dual-track exchange rate system, and China's first stock markets had been formally established in Shanghai and Shenzhen.

The current shape of China's domestic financial system first began to emerge in a period of intense institutional change that lasted from 1978 to 1984.[20] During this time, the PBOC was made separate from the MOF and placed under the direct supervision of the State Council. The State Administration of Foreign Exchange (SAFE) was established under the PBOC to manage and approve distribution of China's foreign exchange reserves. The commercial banking aspects of the PBOC's operations were spun off to establish what would become China's "Big Four" state-owned megabanks: Bank of China, focused on foreign trade and investment financing; Agricultural Bank of China, which emphasized serving the needs of the rural economy; China Construction Bank, specialized in fixed asset investment; and the Industrial and Commercial Bank of China, which, as the last created, took over the mixed remainder of the PBOC's operations in 1984. Other smaller financial intermediaries, such as credit cooperatives and trust and investment companies, proliferated alongside these new institutions and would continue to expand throughout the 1980s. At the same time, and preempting central approval, Shanghai and Shenzhen also began building the institutions needed to establish a domestic stock market.

---

18. Zheng Wang, "Not Rising, But Rejuvenating: The 'Chinese Dream,'" *The Diplomat*, February 5, 2013, http://thediplomat.com/2013/02/chinese-dream-draft/.

19. For a more detailed account of the structure of China's financial system and administrative reforms during this period (on which this section draws heavily), see Franklin Allen, Jun "QJ" Qian, Chenying Zhang, and Mengxin Zhao, *China's Financial System: Opportunities and Challenges*, NBER Working Paper No. 17828 (Cambridge, MA: National Bureau of Economic Research, February 2012), http://www.nber.org/papers/w17828.pdf.

20. For a more comprehensive review of the evolution of the Chinese financial system, see Allen et al., *China's Financial System*.

The institutional reforms that took place during this period produced a dramatic shift in who allocated credit within the Chinese economy: state-owned banks replaced government budget appropriations as the dominant source of firms' investment financing by the early 1980s. However, the new role of banks did little to make the allocation of capital less political. Instead of focusing on commercial considerations, China's banks found themselves struggling to manage competing political objectives. On the one hand, they were required to focus a large share of their lending on supporting nonviable firms threatened by competition. This was needed in order to avoid mass unemployment and maintain stability. On the other hand, central government measures to insulate savers' deposits from the high inflation of the 1980s often resulted in narrow—or even negative—spreads between lending and deposit rates. This led to a steady deterioration of bank balance sheets through the 1980s and into the 1990s. Among other factors, pervasive interference in lending decisions by local party officials (who often controlled the appointments of banks' branch managers) and banks' limited technical capacity for assessing borrower creditworthiness further exacerbated the issue.

The financial reforms undertaken during this period had important positive effects for the development of China's domestic financial system. In particular, the establishment of new institutions patterned on those of a market economy laid the foundation for future rounds of reform. On the international front, China also made progress toward bringing its overvalued official exchange rate more closely in line with market fundamentals through a series of gradual devaluations of the RMB, and allowed the first foreign investors to enter the previously closed Chinese market. At the same time, the growing pains were significant. The inflation that resulted from the surge in lending and new money creation during the 1980s was a major factor behind the unrest that triggered the Tiananmen Square protests of 1989 and the subsequent period of political retrenchment. Following Tiananmen, financial reforms (and economic reform in general) were largely put on hold until after Deng Xiaoping embarked on his famous Southern Tour in 1992.

## FINANCIAL REFORM DEEPENS: 1992–2005

The period from 1992 to 2005 saw Chinese leaders push deep and painful reforms that transformed the country's ailing financial system, strengthened its market orientation, and laid the foundations for a decade of rapid economic growth. On the domestic front, reformers in Beijing, led by Premier Zhu Rongji, oversaw the recapitalization and public listing of China's ailing Big Four banks, and introduced reforms to strengthen their subsequent performance and profit orientation. The PBOC was restructured to improve its surveillance capacity, and new regulatory institutions, including the CBRC, CIRC, and China Securities Regulatory Commission (CSRC), were established to improve financial regulation and support broadening of China's financial system. After earning official government approval in 1991, the capitalization of the Shanghai and Shenzhen stock markets grew remarkably (particularly through 2000). Bond markets were arguably the only aspect of China's financial system that did not experience significant development during this period.

The most significant financial system reforms that took place during this period were almost certainly the start of interest rate liberalization (in 1996) and the massive overhaul of China's banking system, which, as discussed previously, had become increasingly impaired by a rapidly growing stock of nonperforming loans (NPLs) over the course of the 1990s.

By 1998, the extent of China's bad loans were estimated at as much as 40 to 50 percent of total lending and roughly 30 percent of GDP.[21] Responding to the shock of the Asian Financial Crisis, Premier Zhu Rongji oversaw an ambitious strategy that recapitalized China's banks, transferred their bad loans to government-backed asset management companies, forced aggressive restructuring of operations (including significant cuts in staff), and invited foreign banks to take equity stakes in the Big Four as strategic investors as a means of introducing international best practices in technology and management. In addition to these and other measures designed to strengthen banks' commercial orientation, Beijing also began implementing a policy of financial repression to protect bank profitability and support a high rate of investment. This was, in effect, a reversal of the policy of the previous decade, which had sacrificed bank balance sheets for the sake of protecting depositors. While effective in its time, this policy shift would contribute to deepening the macroeconomic imbalances that China is still struggling to address today.

China also undertook significant reforms to bring its exchange rate more in line with market fundamentals during this period. In 1994, Beijing devalued the RMB by 33 percent and eliminated the dual-track exchange rate system. Over the next three years, it allowed the RMB to gradually appreciate to 8.28 yuan per dollar by September 1997. In response to the Asian financial crisis, the RMB was then repegged to the dollar until 2005. During this period, the PBOC intervened consistently to maintain the peg, while allowing consistent real appreciation (due to the consistent inflation differential between the United States and China).[22]

Another important outcome of this period of intensive reform was the continued modernization of China's financial regulatory apparatus. By the end of 2003, the PBOC had undergone structural reform to reduce the influence of provincial officials over its branch offices, and been stripped of its functions as a bank regulator, strengthening its institutional orientation as a "pure" central bank (though it remained under the direction of the State Council). The PBOC's bank supervisory responsibilities (and around 200 members of its staff) were then transferred to the CBRC, a new ministry-level body that officially opened its doors in April 2003 with a mandate to oversee regulation of the banking

---

21. Yukon Huang and Canyon Bosler, *China's Debt Dilemma: Deleveraging While Generating Growth* (Washington, DC: Carnegie Endowment for International Peace, September 2014), http://carnegieendowment.org/files/china_debt_dilemma.pdf; for a thorough review of China's financial challenges at the time, see Bank for International Settlements (BIS), *Strengthening the Banking System in China: Issues and Experience*, BIS Policy Papers No. 7 (Basel: BIS, October 1999), http://www.bis.org/publ/plcy07.htm.

22. Wayne M. Morrison and Marc Labonte, "China's Currency Policy: An Analysis of the Economic Issues," Congressional Research Service, July 22, 2013, https://www.fas.org/sgp/crs/row/RS21625.pdf.

system.[23] This period also saw the creation of the CSRC (in 1992) and the CIRC (in 1998), such that by end-2003 all the formal structures of China's current financial policymaking apparatus were in place.

At the same time, another lesser-known party organization was at work behind the scenes, managing reforms designed to use improved personnel management to reassert the party's control over the financial system. The Central Financial Work Commission (CFWC), established in mid-1998 with the backing of Zhu and headed by then vice premier Wen Jiabao, was responsible for the appraisal and appointment of thousands of senior executives in national financial institutions (ostensibly chosen for their technical skills and party loyalty).[24] Until its dissolution in 2003, the CFWC played a major role in recentralizing party control and supervision of bank managers within the national institutions that, at the time, held roughly 80 percent of financial industry assets in China.[25]

## KEY FEATURES OF THE FINANCIAL SYSTEM AT THE START OF THE XI ADMINISTRATION

From 2005 through end-2012, China's financial reform process stalled. The Zhu-era reforms had restored China's major financial institutions to positions of strength, and the Hu-Wen administration directed its focus elsewhere. Meanwhile, with net interest margins protected by the PBOC-set deposit rate ceiling and other controls, China's major commercial banks were able to improve their profitability without significantly raising their lending standards or risk assessment capacity. Instead, they concentrated on lending to state-owned firms (mainly in industrial sectors), which enjoyed implicit government backing and could pledge large stocks of physical collateral. The development of China's direct financing channels, such as stock and bond markets, also stalled. However, this period did see the growth of a large shadow-banking sector, which expanded rapidly following the financial crisis. On the external front, the RMB appreciated almost 40 percent against the dollar in real terms from 2005 through 2012, even as China's foreign exchange reserves expanded at double-digit rates (a product of the PBOC's efforts to limit the rate and extent of appreciation through intervention).

At the start of the Xi administration and through the present, banks remain the primary source of credit within the Chinese economy, but the financial system has also become significantly more diverse and complicated with time.[26] As of end-2012, bank credit was equal to 128 percent of GDP, with the Big Four (plus Communication Bank of China, the country's fifth-largest lender) accounting for around half of this lending. Joint-stock com-

23. Barry Naughton, "Government Reorganization: Liu Mingkang and Financial Restructuring," *China Leadership Monitor*, no. 7 (Summer 2003), http://www.hoover.org/sites/default/files/uploads/documents/clm7_bn.pdf.

24. For a more thorough account of this process, see Sebastian Heilmann, "Regulatory Innovation by Leninist Means: Communist Party Supervision in China's Financial Industry," *China Quarterly* 181 (March 2005), http://journals.cambridge.org/action/displayAbstract?fromPage=online&aid=290062.

25. Notably, the CFWC left control over appointments at local financial institutions to local party committees.

26. This section and many of the statistics contained herein draw from the thorough and highly accessible work of Douglas Elliott and Kai Yan, *The Chinese Financial System*.

mercial banks were the second-largest source of bank credit, followed by rural financial institutions and city commercial banks. Despite China's pledges to open the financial sector to greater foreign participation as part of its WTO accession package, foreign banks had less than a 2 percent market share as of end-2013.[27]

Political influence over the banking system remains extensive at the national and local levels and continues to exert an influence on bank lending patterns (though the precise extent of this influence is debated). The heads of China's largest banks are appointed by the CCOD, and enjoy ministerial or vice-ministerial rank within the state system, in addition to whatever party rank they might hold. Local governments continue to exert both active and passive influence on bank lending decisions (though their direct influence appears to be lessening with time). For example, a loan officer at a local branch of a national bank is likely to be more inclined to lend to a local SOE, which enjoys the implicit guarantee of the local government, rather than lend to a private enterprise, which might default and harm the loan officer's career.

While efforts are under way to further develop China's domestic stock and bond markets, these channels for direct financing remain significantly underdeveloped relative to the banking system. At the start of the Xi administration, bonds accounted for credit equivalent to only 41 percent of GDP, and China's stock market capitalization was roughly 45 percent of GDP. The reasons for this underdevelopment are many and varied, ranging from the complicated regulatory framework surrounding bond issuance to the limited rights shareholders can exercise over major listed companies (most of which are least partly state owned). However, Chinese leaders have identified the strengthening of direct financing channels as an important priority of future financial reforms in order to improve the ability of China's financial system to serve the needs of the real economy.

Even as these financing channels have been slow to develop, China's tight regulatory controls have had the side effect of spawning a thriving shadow-banking sector, which grew up particularly in the aftermath of the global financial crisis and accounted for 42 percent of new credit creation in 2012.[28] This has had the important effect of magnifying the complexity and opacity of the Chinese financial system, and has been a major source of concern for Chinese financial regulators for some time.[29] On the other hand, it has also been tolerated, and even encouraged to some degree, as a means of introducing more market pricing of risk and creating competition for deposits without lifting existing controls. Another more recent, but rapidly growing, source of competition is China's Internet finance platforms. In comparison with established players, these institutions are small,

27. "Lenders of little resort," *The Economist*, June 28, 2014, http://www.economist.com/news/finance-and-economics/21605920-china-enticing-elusive-market-foreign-banks-lenders-little-resort.

28. Borst, "Flying Blind."

29. Along with other aspects of China's overall financial deepening, the growth of the shadow banking sector has also reduced the effectiveness of the PBOC's quantitative tools for overseeing the money supply's rate of expansion and encouraging its gradual and ongoing shift toward more market-based tools for liquidity management. See Wei Liao and Sampawende J.-A. Tapsoba, *China's Monetary Policy and Interest Rate Liberalization: Lessons from International Experiences*, IMF Working Paper No. WP/14/75 (Washington, DC: IMF, May 2014), https://www.imf.org/external/pubs/ft/wp/2014/wp1475.pdf.

but by intensifying competition for deposits at the margin they have the potential to exert a powerful effect on bank behavior moving forward.

## China's Financial Regulatory Institutions

This section covers the basic structure of the Chinese financial regulatory and supervisory system and provides brief outlines of the responsibilities and histories of some of the main functional ministries. It focuses on the formal institutions of the state, but this is not to suggest the party is absent. Through the Central Committee Organization Department and the *nomenklatura* system, the party controls appointments at the major banks and regulatory institutions. Under the Xi administration, the CFELSG and its office staff have also exercised greater control over the Chinese financial regulatory system and the process of financial reform.

The State Council has formal authority for supervising China's financial regulatory apparatus, and major decisions regarding monetary policy or financial regulation must be approved by the State Council or its 10-member executive committee. The main financial regulators—the PBOC, MOF, CBRC, CSRC, and CIRC—are all ministry-ranked agencies and members of the State Council. They are entitled to attend its full meetings and may be called to executive committee meetings as necessary. SAFE, as a vice-ministerial agency under the PBOC, is not officially a member of the State Council. While the NPC nominally has responsibility for oversight of the State Council and must approve any major legislative changes, in practice it is a rubber stamp, lacking the time or capacity to effectively perform this function.

### PEOPLE'S BANK OF CHINA (PBOC)

Established in 1949, the PBOC functioned as both a central and commercial bank under the control of the MOF until 1978, when it was established as an independent agency under the State Council and given full ministerial rank.[30] Over the subsequent years, its commercial banking operations were gradually spun off, and the scope of the PBOC's mandate narrowed to reduce its involvement in commercial operations (although it retained responsibility for bank oversight). In 1998, a round of structural reforms reorganized the PBOC along lines similar to the U.S. Federal Reserve, consolidating its provincial operations into nine regional branches. This was designed to reduce the influence of provincial officials on policy implementation.[31] In March 2003, yet another bureaucratic reshuffle stripped the PBOC of its responsibility for bank oversight, allowing it to focus it attentions on the conduct of monetary policy and maintenance of overall financial stability.[32]

30. Allen et al., *China's Financial System*, 5.

31. Arthur J. Rolnick, "Interview with Ping Xie," *The Region*, December 1, 2013, https://www.minneapolisfed.org/publications/the-region/interview-with-ping-xie.

32. Ibid.

While not formally independent (being under the supervision of the State Council), the PBOC and its staff have earned a reputation for strong technical capacity and effectiveness in the conduct of monetary policy. As an institution, the PBOC has long advocated in favor of a more liberalized domestic financial system, a more flexible exchange rate in line with market fundamentals, and a more open capital account (taking into account internal and external conditions). These views are in particular associated with longtime PBOC governor Zhou Xiaochuan, who has served as the bank's head since December 2002 (he is also secretary of the PBOC's party committee).[33] In late 2013, Zhou was revealed to be a member of both the CDRLSG and the CFELSG, illustrating his continued importance in the Xi administration's system of economic policymaking. The PBOC successfully argued in favor of avoiding broad monetary stimulus measures for the first two years of the Xi administration to promote restructuring, staving off calls from the NDRC (among others) for a loosening of rates.[34]

The PBOC conducts monetary policy through its control over the required reserve ratio for banks, the discount rate for interbank lending, and open market operations. In contrast to the U.S. Federal Reserve and central banks in other advanced economies, the PBOC has often used the required reserve ratio as its primary tool for adjusting the money supply, and makes comparatively heavy use of quantity-based targets (such as M2) for monitoring money supply growth. For the first two years of the Xi administration, the PBOC largely eschewed broad easing measures, instead making more targeted efforts to encourage the flow of credit to priority sectors, such as by making credit lines selectively available to banks focused on lending to agricultural concerns. The goal of these operations was to ease selectively, limiting further borrowing by overleveraged SOEs or investment in overcapacity sectors while avoiding a sharp overall slowdown. This reflected the PBOC's general concerns about structural bias in how the Chinese financial system allocates capital.[35] As the economy struggled in the latter half of 2014 and early 2015, the PBOC changed its approach, cutting its benchmark interest rate twice in an effort to stabilize the economy. At the same time, demonstrating its commitment to continuing the gradual process of interest rate liberalization, the PBOC paired both rate cuts with increases in the benchmark lending rate.[36]

---

33. Bob Davis and Lingling Wei, "China's Central Banker Leads Push to Overhaul Economy," *Wall Street Journal*, November 5, 2013, http://www.wsj.com/articles/SB10001424052702304200804579164003669215172.

34. Lingling Wei and Bob Davis, "China's Central Bank Prevails in Policy Battles Over Economic Future," *Wall Street Journal*, June 8, 2014, http://www.wsj.com/articles/chinas-central-bank-prevails-in-policy-battles-over-economic-future-1402270855.

35. In February 2015, the PBOC did announce an across-the-board cut in its required reserve ratio, with an additional cut for city commercial banks and certain rural commercial banks, as well as the Agricultural Development Bank of China. This reflected both deepening concern about China's overall growth and a continued effort to encourage lending to priority sectors. See Xiaoqing Pi, "China Joins Global-Easing Wave with Bank Reserve Ratio Cut," Bloomberg, February 4, 2015, http://www.bloomberg.com/news/articles/2015-02-04/china-cuts-banks-reserve-ratio-in-liquidity-move-to-spur-growth.

36. Jing Yang, "China's central bank announces long-awaited rate cut to boost economy," *South China Morning Post*, February 28, 2015, http://www.scmp.com/news/china/article/1725806/china-cut-benchmark-interest-rates-25-basis-points-pboc-announces.

## STATE ADMINISTRATION OF FOREIGN EXCHANGE (SAFE)

Established in 1978, SAFE is a vice-ministerial agency under the PBOC,[37] charged with the management of China's more than $3.5 trillion in foreign exchange reserves.[38] SAFE's core functions are foreign exchange management, maintenance of balance of payments statistics, and the oversight of foreign exchange transactions (as well as the issuance of related regulations). It is also responsible for managing the qualified foreign institutional investors program. While the Chinese government does not officially acknowledge SAFE as such, it also functions in many ways like a sovereign wealth fund, and is the world's third-largest in terms of assets-under-management.[39] It oversees fund management arms located in four major financial centers around the world: Singapore, Hong Kong, London, and New York. The current head of SAFE is Administrator Yi Gang, who also serves concurrently as a deputy governor of the PBOC and, as of April 2014, a deputy director of the office of the CFELSG—effectively the secretariat for implementing the current leadership's reform agenda.

## CHINA BANKING REGULATORY COMMISSION (CBRC)

The CBRC was formally established in 2003, as a ministry-ranked agency. It holds broad responsibility for supervising and regulating China's banking system and ensuring that the interests of depositors and consumers are protected. The CBRC was initially staffed by personnel transferred from the PBOC and the now-defunct CFWC.[40] Under the leadership of its first director, Liu Mingkang (2003–2011), the CBRC earned a reputation for taking a proactive approach to limiting the accumulation of risk in the banking sector, even when doing so came at the cost of tighter credit conditions.[41]

Unlike the PBOC, the CBRC is organized along provincial lines, which, along with its necessarily close working relationships with China's banks, has led to some concerns over its independence. The CBRC's comparatively cautious attitude toward financial liberalization has also reportedly led to disagreements with the more liberally minded PBOC and impaired the effectiveness of a financial regulatory coordinating body established in August 2013.[42] Since 2011, the CBRC has been headed by Shang Fulin, a member of the 18th CCP Central Committee and an experienced technocrat who served previously as the head of the CSRC, as president of the Agricultural Bank of China, and, in the late 1990s, as a deputy governor of the PBOC.

---

37. Despite being an agency under the PBOC, the relationship has not always been harmonious. For example, see Pete Sweeney, "Insight: China turf war over yuan reform rattles foreign firms," Reuters, August 4, 2013, http://www.reuters.com/article/2013/08/04/us-china-economy-yuan-idUSBRE9730B220130804.

38. Allen et al., *China's Financial System*.

39. Iacob N. Koch-Weser and Owen D. Haacke, *China Investment Corporation: Recent Developments in Performance, Strategy, and Governance* (Washington, DC: U.S.-China Economic and Security Review Commission, June 2013), http://www.uscc.gov/sites/default/files/Research/China%20Investment%20Corporation_Staff%20Report_0.pdf.

40. Naughton, "Government Reorganization."

41. Ibid.

42. For example, see Jamil Anderlini, "Fear of crisis intensifies China's political battles," *Financial Times*, April 9, 2014, http://www.ft.com/intl/cms/s/0/b28aed1e-bfc6-11e3-b6e8-00144feabdc0.html?siteedition=intl.

## MINISTRY OF FINANCE (MOF)

Established in 1949, MOF is a ministry-ranked agency and sits on the full State Council. It is responsible for macroeconomic surveillance and for compiling the national annual budget. While not directly involved in the collection of taxes, which falls within the purview of the State Administration of Taxation, MOF is responsible for managing the vital system of fiscal transfers between central and local governments (though it does not determine their distribution).[43] It is also an important source of data used for benchmarking economic activity, including closely watched statistics related to central government debt and borrowing. Through share holdings in major commercial banks and its control over the Central Huijin Company, MOF is loosely involved in financial regulation, though it does not exercise direct regulatory authority over said banks.[44] It is also in charge of China's official sovereign wealth fund, the China Investment Corporation.[45]

For much of reform and opening, MOF experienced a gradual decline in importance, as progressive rounds of reform split its once-extensive portfolio across several more specialized agencies. As a result, it is often noted (even on the State Council's own website) that MOF exercises relatively little authority when compared to its international counterparts.[46] Other Chinese ministries have responsibility for key elements of economic policy: the NDRC for macroeconomic management; separate commissions for banking, insurance, and securities regulation; and the PBOC for monitoring of money markets. However, today MOF is playing an increasingly important role. Under Minister Lou Jiwei, a highly respected technocrat who also serves on the Comprehensively Deepening Reform and Finance and Economics central leading small groups, MOF has developed, and is now in charge of implementing, a much-touted comprehensive fiscal reform plan.[47] This plan, which has received endorsement from the CDRLSG and been consistently stressed by the Xi leadership as a top priority, is expected to be a major focus of reform in 2015.[48]

## NATIONAL DEVELOPMENT AND REFORM COMMISSION (NDRC)

The NDRC was the most powerful ministry under the State Council during the Hu-Wen administration, responsible for oversight of many key prices and investment approvals processes, as well as coordination of the national five-year planning process (and more). Established in its current form in 2003, through the merging of the State Council Office for Restructuring the Economic System and part of the State Economic and Trade Commission,

43. Yuen Yuen Ang, "Centralizing Treasury Management in China: The Rationale of the Central Reformers," *Public Administration and Development* 29, issue 4 (October 2009).

44. Elliott and Yan, *The Chinese Financial System.*

45. Itself a fascinating agency, the history of which provides a useful illustration of the interministerial disputes common within the Chinese bureaucracy. For details of this, see Koch-Weser and Haacke, *China Investment Corporation.*

46. Ministry of Finance of the People's Republic of China State Council website, http://english.gov.cn/state_council/2014/09/09/content_281474986284115.htm.

47. Barry Naughton, "'Deepening Reform': The Organization and the Emerging Strategy," *China Leadership Monitor*, no. 44 (Summer 2014), http://www.hoover.org/sites/default/files/research/docs/clm44bn.pdf.

48. For details, see Barry Naughton, "It's All in the Execution: Struggling with the Reform Agenda," *China Leadership Monitor*, no. 45 (Fall 2014), http://www.hoover.org/sites/default/files/research/docs/clm45bn-its_all_in_the_execution-struggling_with_the_reform_agenda.pdf.

the NDRC traces its origins to the powerful State Planning Commission, a central planning authority established in 1952.[49] Even as the process of "growing out of the plan" had gradually reduced the authority of its precursor agencies throughout the course of "reform and opening," the NDRC was a force to be reckoned with during the first decade of the new millennium. Often referred to as the "mini–State Council," the NDRC was designed to help the State Council coordinate China's massive bureaucracy, with many of its subdivisions corresponding to the remits of other State Council ministries.[50]

However, by the end of the Hu-Wen administration, the NDRC had come to be viewed as the primary bureaucratic obstacle to reform, rather than the organizer and enabler its name suggested.[51] As a result, under the Xi-Li leadership, the NDRC's power has been sharply curtailed. Many of its administrative approval items have been eliminated, and its coordination role is reportedly much diminished. While it is still the only ministry-level agency with four minister-level officials in leadership positions, the personnel chosen for these positions reflects the new leadership's determination to monitor and control the agency rather than to empower it.[52] Current director Xu Shaoshi is an outsider to the NDRC, having served previously as Minister of Land and Resources, while minister-ranked vice director Liu He is a close confidante of Xi Jinping and head of the secretariat of the CFELSG. This has resulted in the NDRC becoming much more closely aligned with the priorities of the current leadership, both as a result of its own internal leadership change and in an effort to maintain its relevance through a new period of more market-oriented reform.

## MINISTRY OF COMMERCE (MOFCOM)

In 2003, MOFCOM was created out of a merger of the State Economic and Trade Commission and State Development Planning Commission into the Ministry of Foreign Trade and Economic Co-Operation. MOFCOM is a ministry-level agency that serves as the State Council's interface for international economic cooperation, overseeing policy toward foreign trade and direct investment, as well as the negotiation of bilateral and multilateral trade and investment agreements. The current minister of commerce is Gao Hucheng, a member of the 18th Central Committee.

The Ministry consists of 29 internal departments (both functional and regional) that administer a collection of offices domestically and overseas, as well as affiliate bureaus. Its responsibilities also include oversight of industry trade associations and institutes, as well as chambers of commerce. Relative to other China's bureaucratic agencies, MOFCOM has a reputation for being liberal on matters related to trade and foreign investment. However,

49. Peter Martin, "The Humbling of the NDRC," *China Brief* 14, no. 5 (March 7, 2014), http://www.jamestown.org/uploads/media/China_Brief_Vol_14_Issue_5_-_Copy__2__01.pdf.

50. Lance L. P. Gore, "China's 'Mini–State Council': National Development and Reform Commission," EAI Background Brief No. 614, East Asian Institute, April 8, 2011, http://www.eai.nus.edu.sg/BB614.pdf.

51. Victoria Ruan, "Reform underway for China's top economic planning agency," *South China Morning Post*, December 3, 2013, http://www.scmp.com/news/china/article/1370795/reform-underway-chinas-top-economic-planning-agency.

52. Martin, "The Humbling of the NDRC."

in the past it has also been a staunch opponent of RMB appreciation, particularly in the years immediately following the global financial crisis, reflecting its role as a champion of China's export-oriented industries.[53]

# Case Studies

The following three case studies were undertaken to illuminate the processes and institutions of Chinese decisionmaking in a key area of economic reform. Each case was chosen to provide an example of policymaking in one of the three primary areas of financial reform discussed earlier: interest rate deregulation, exchange rate marketization, and capital account liberalization. In order to illustrate how the Xi administration's approach to financial reform has evolved (and, in some ways, remained consistent), each of the case studies covers a different time period.

The first case reviews the June 2013 interbank market shock, wherein the PBOC engineered a dramatic liquidity crunch in order to contain growing risks in the interbank market as part of the overall shift toward greater interest rate deregulation. The second case study covers the widening of the RMB trading band in the first quarter of 2014, and the actions undertaken by the PBOC to discipline speculators and create its preferred conditions for a more market-determined exchange rate. The third case study reviews the evolution of the Shanghai FTZ from its conception and opening through the present, with emphasis on reforms within the zone to promote greater capital account liberalization.

Following the case studies, a concluding section provides an overview assessment of the Xi administration's approach to financial reform thus far.

## THE JUNE 2013 INTERBANK MARKET SHOCK

In June 2013, China's interbank markets seized up in response to an unexpected withdrawal of liquidity. This represented a deliberate effort by the PBOC, acting with the private support of top Chinese leaders but without the full knowledge or endorsement of other regulators, to force banks to improve their liquidity management and crack down on the excess credit creation then taking place through interbank channels. If left unchecked, these problems would raise the risks to stability posed by greater interest rate liberalization. Coming only eight months into the new leadership's term, the events of June 2013 illustrate many of the policymaking patterns that have since come to characterize the first two years of the Xi administration: rapid, opaque, informal, and centralized decisionmaking; lack of coordination or information-sharing among functional ministries; and a willingness to use untested and unorthodox tools in the service of policy objectives.

---

53. Charles W. Freeman III and Wen Yin Yuan, *China's Exchange Rate Politics* (Washington, DC: CSIS, June 2011), http://csis.org/files/publication/110615_Freeman_ChinaExchangeRatePolitics_Web.pdf.

*Sequence of Events*

Since the global financial crisis, China's debt-to-GDP ratio has grown rapidly, even as credit has gone to increasingly unproductive uses. Over this same period, the Chinese financial system has become ever more complex and, to a large extent, opaque. This owes in part to the rapid growth of shadow banking, shorthand for a slew of nontraditional lending activities that in 2012 accounted for 42 percent of new domestic credit creation.[54] In the lead up to June 2013, these two trends of excess credit growth (accompanied by poor liquidity management on the part of China's banks) and an expanding shadow banking sector represented major concerns for Chinese financial regulators seeking ways to move toward eventual interest rate liberalization without triggering major financial instability.

Continuing the trends of previous years, the rate of credit growth reached record highs in the first half of 2013, and the share of shadow banking in total social financing (an aggregate measure of lending activity) continued to rise. Contributing to the rate of increase was a combined capital and financial account surplus of $102 billion in the first quarter, which helped to create excess domestic liquidity.[55] Regulators responded beginning in March, with the CBRC, PBOC, and SAFE issuing a succession of public warnings and new regulations designed to slow down credit growth.[56] The CBRC in particular warned banks to be careful in engaging in shadow banking activities, urging them to "serve the real economy" and "stay risk averse.[57] But during the first weeks of June, it seemed clear these warnings were not producing the desired effects. Credit in the first 10 days of the month grew at a rate that, according to the PBOC, "had never been seen in history," with 70 percent of that growth taking place through precisely the short-term, off-balance-sheet channels that were regulators' particular area of concern.[58]

However, the PBOC had in fact already begun to act. In January 2013, it had quietly announced the establishment of two new tools, Standing Liquidity Operations (SLO) and the Standing Lending Facility (SLF), which would enable it to conduct targeted, short-term

54. Borst, "Flying Blind."

55. Gabriel Wildau, "China targets hot money inflows with new forex rules," Reuters, May 6, 2013, http://www.reuters.com/article/2013/05/06/us-china-economy-forex-idUSBRE94500Y20130506.

56. For example, see Grace Zhu, "China Regulators Move to Restrain Lending," *Wall Street Journal*, February 5, 2013, http://www.wsj.com/articles/SB10001424127887324445904578283413907968812; China Banking Regulatory Commission, "Notice of the China Banking Regulatory Commission on Relevant Issues concerning Regulating the Investment Operation of Wealth Management Business of Commercial Banks," *Lawinfochina*, March 25, 2013, http://www.lawinfochina.com/display.aspx?lib=law&id=13829&CGid; State Administration of Foreign Exchange, "Notice of the State Administration of Foreign Exchange on Issues concerning Strengthening the Administration of Foreign Exchange Capital Inflows," *Lawinfochina*, May 5, 2013, http://www.lawinfochina.com/display.aspx?lib=law&id=13294.

57. See Shang Fulin, "Opening Speech by CBRC Chairman SHANG Fulin at the 18th International Conference of Banking Supervisors," China Banking Regulatory Commission (CBRC), September 24, 2014, http://www.cbrc.gov.cn/EngdocView.do?docID=A0BD73C45F0A42A29D5FABE9EB4B7F3B; CBRC, "Guiding Opinions on Banking Services Should Serve Real Economy," in *China Banking Regulatory Commission: 2013 Annual Report* (Beijing: CBRC, September 2014), http://www.cbrc.gov.cn/chinese/files/2014/A2726BEBE1AA406BB5CAC4ADA3875D35.pdf.

58. Lingling Wei and Bob Davis, "Inside China's Bank-Rate Missteps," *Wall Street Journal*, July 2, 2013, http://www.wsj.com/articles/SB10001424127887324251504578579292237914344.

easing operations in the event of stress in interbank markets.[59] Beginning in May, it had also begun withdrawing liquidity from the financial system through repurchase operations and the issuance of large volumes of central bank bills.[60]

This came in advance of a time of cyclical stress in the Chinese financial system, when the June overlap of the annual Dragon Boat holiday and quarter-end regulatory checks lead to an upswing in demand for deposits. In past years, the PBOC had reliably provided additional short-term liquidity to cope with this surge. By instead moving policy in the exact opposite direction, without announcement and contrary to expectations, it amplified the effect of relatively modest tightening measures on overall conditions. Poor liquidity management was another major factor. Through the interbank markets, China's largest banks were net lenders to smaller banks, which were creating maturity mismatches by borrowing short term and using the funds to finance longer term lending.[61] The first sign that the drawdown was beginning to bite came on June 5, when (later confirmed) rumors broke that China Everbright Bank, the country's 11th largest lender, had experienced a technical default in the interbank market.[62] The next day, an auction of government debt overseen by the Ministry of Finance came in undersubscribed.[63] This led the overnight Shanghai Interbank Offer Rate (SHIBOR) to begin to spike upward, closing above 8 percent on June 7.[64]

As these stresses intensified, market confusion mounted and many smaller banks that had been borrowing short term in the interbank market began experiencing severe funding difficulties. On June 14, a second MOF bond auction came in undersubscribed.[65] To this point, the PBOC had not acknowledged that anything out of the ordinary was under way and had made no specific public comment on liquidity conditions. Privately, staff were considering how to convey the PBOC's view to the market: that overall liquidity was sufficient, provided large banks stopped hoarding deposits and lent to smaller lenders experiencing shortages. After staff reaffirmed this assessment at an internal PBOC meeting on June 19, the State Council ratified its decision that same day and Premier Li Keqiang gave it

---

59. Monetary Policy Analysis Group of the People's Bank of China (PBOC), "China Monetary Policy Report: Quarter One, 2013," PBOC, May 9, 2013, http://www.pbc.gov.cn/image_public/UserFiles/english/upload/File/13Q1MPR_EN_%5BafterNancy%5D1.pdf.

60. For a more technical account of this and other aspects of the June shock, see Daniel H. Rosen and Beibei Bao, "China's Interbank Squeeze: Understanding the 2013 Drama and Anticipating 2014," Rhodium Group, January 22, 2014, http://rhg.com/notes/chinas-interbank-squeeze-understanding-the-2013-drama-and-anticipating-2014.

61. This situation was in large part an outgrowth of the stimulus package China deployed in response to the financial crisis. Many smaller banks had lent in support of long-term infrastructure and development projects, but faced short-term repayment obligations, which they managed through borrowing on the interbank market.

62. Dinny McMahon and Grace Zhu, "China Everbright Admits to Interbank-Loan Default," *Wall Street Journal*, December 16, 2013, http://blogs.wsj.com/chinarealtime/2013/12/16/china-everbright-admits-to-interbank-loan-default/.

63. William Kazer and Shen Hong, "China Cash Crunch Squeezes Banks," *Wall Street Journal*, June 14, 2013, http://www.wsj.com/articles/SB10001424127887324188604578545184149408090.

64. Mamta Badkar, "Yesterday's Huge Chinese Interest Rate Spike Has People Freaked Out about a Looming Credit Crisis," *Business Insider*, June 7, 2013, http://www.businessinsider.com/what-shibors-surge-says-about-chinas-financial-system-2013-6.

65. Kazer and Hong, "China Cash Crunch Squeezes Banks."

public voice.[66] Rather than reassuring rattled markets, in his remarks Li urged banks to "make better use of existing credit" and "step up efforts to contain financial risks"—in effect, giving the top leadership's public endorsement of the PBOC's efforts.[67]

In response, interbank rates spiked even higher, as markets interpreted the decision to mean that no relief would be forthcoming. Later that same day, the unexpected announcement of the U.S. Federal Reserve's "taper" added another major source of uncertainty.[68] On June 20, the following day, the crisis peaked: a rumor emerged in Shanghai that Bank of China, one of China's Big Four banks, had experienced a temporary default. This rumor was then picked up in the widely circulated 21st Century Business Herald.[69] Despite Bank of China's having issued a swift denial via its Sina Weibo social media account, the overnight SHIBOR subsequently spiked above 30 percent in intraday trading. Both Bank of China and Industrial and Commercial Bank of China then announced they would temporarily halt lending. Behind the scenes, Vice Premier Ma Kai responded by ordering an investigation into the source of the Bank of China rumor.[70]

By this time, the PBOC was facing widespread criticism for being irresponsible in its management of the interbank market, and for its perceived refusal to ease liquidity conditions.[71] In fact, it had once again already begun to act.

Following the State Council and Premier Li's statements on June 19, PBOC officials had called in a number of banks to privately alert them that they would be receiving injections of fresh funds (via the aforementioned SLO)—and to warn them to use these funds wisely.[72] However, these private assurances were insufficient to stem the market's panic. A public statement issued on June 24, asserting that there was sufficient liquidity in the financial system, would prove similarly ineffective. It was only on June 25, when the PBOC issued an official statement that it would take steps to "safeguard stability," that it began to make headway.[73] While not reversing its earlier stance that there was sufficient liquidity and continuing to call on large banks to act as market stabilizers, the PBOC's insertion of this key language (along with public statements from senior officials) signaled to markets that the worst of the crisis was over. A similar statement by the State Council released the

66. Wei and Davis, "Inside China's Bank-Rate Missteps."

67. It was also an accurate assessment of aggregate liquidity conditions. Data available to the PBOC showed that the aggregate level of reserves available in the system was on the order of 1.5 trillion RMB. It was the allocation of these reserves that was the source of stress: larger banks began hoarding and refused to lend to smaller banks, which had borrowed short term and were facing significant liquidity shortages.

68. Agustino Fontevecchia, "China's Central Bank Is Engineering a Liquidity Crunch to Tackle the Shadow Banking System," *Forbes*, June 20, 2013, http://www.forbes.com/sites/afontevecchia/2013/06/20/chinas-central-bank-is-engineering-a-liquidity-crunch-to-tackle-the-shadow-banking-system/.

69. "Bank denies default allegations," China.org.cn, June 21, 2013, http://www.china.org.cn/business/2013-06/21/content_29184731.htm.

70. Wei and Davis, "Inside China's Bank-Rate Missteps."

71. Bob Davis and Shen Hong, "China Faces Fallout of Self-Made Cash Crisis," *Wall Street Journal*, June 21, 2013, http://www.wsj.com/articles/SB10001424127887323300004578558963563872992.

72. Ibid.

73. Xin Zhou, "PBOC Says It Will Ensure Stability of China Money Market," Bloomberg, June 26, 2013, http://www.bloomberg.com/news/articles/2013-06-25/china-s-liquidity-risks-are-controllable-pboc-official-says.

following day provided further reassurance, and rates subsequently began to return to more normal levels.

### *Aftermath and Implications*

Following the crisis, many reports suggested that the incident was the result of PBOC mismanagement, which had allowed liquidity conditions to get out of hand, and suggested that some form of punishment for its leadership would likely result.[74] This both misinterpreted the origins of the crisis and failed to anticipate its subsequent impact. While the PBOC underestimated the severity of the market's response (and could not have anticipated the amplifying effect of the Fed's surprise "taper" announcement), it had acted with the knowledge and endorsement of top leaders in response to what the PBOC, and other regulators, agreed was a major problem: excessive credit growth and risk taking in the interbank market, coupled with an insensitivity of financial market players to regulators' prior warnings. Despite having acted without the support—and evidence from interviews with regulators suggests without even the knowledge—of its fellow ministries, it was the assessment of top leaders as to the PBOC's effectiveness and the consequences of the crunch that ultimately mattered.

In many respects, the shock was a success and appears to have been judged as such. As a June 26 Xinhua commentary put it, "It takes pains to get through the liquidity crunch, but it also paves [the] way for future gains."[75] Credit growth via interbank markets slowed in the second half of 2013, and interbank market rates remained on average 50 percent above historical levels through April 2014.[76] Defying expectations that it had lost face with Zhongnanhai, the leadership subsequently placed the PBOC in charge of a new financial regulatory coordinating body announced in August 2013.[77] In a further show of support, following the Third Plenum that November, PBOC Governor Zhou was revealed as a member of both the Comprehensively Deepening Reform and Central Finance and Economics leading small groups. PBOC policy preferences have also continued to hold sway in terms of outcomes:[78] even in the face of an ongoing slowdown in economic growth, leaders have

---

74. Jamil Anderlini, "Fear of crisis intensifies China's political battles," *Financial Times*, April 9, 2014, http://www.ft.com/intl/cms/s/0/b28aed1e-bfc6-11e3-b6e8-00144feabdc0.html?siteedition=intl.

75. Liu Jie, "Commentary: No pains, no gains for China's economy," Xinhua, June 26, 2013, http://news.xinhuanet.com/english/indepth/2013-06/26/c_132489507.htm.

76. The impact of the shock in curtailing the use of interbank funding to fuel shadow banking activities also created a window for policymakers to generate an effective regulatory response. In May 2014, the PBOC, CBRC, CSRC, CIRC, and SAFE jointly released Document 127, designed to crack down on the regulatory arbitrage that had been so problematic in the lead-up to June. This had the effect of further discouraging abuse of the interbank markets, though the size of the shadow banking sector has continued to grow at a rate faster than GDP (amounting to 71 percent of GDP at the end of 2014, up from 66 percent at the end of 2013, according to Moody's).

77. Bettina Wassener and Chris Buckley, "New Chinese Agency to Increase Financial Coordination," *New York Times*, August 20, 2013, http://www.nytimes.com/2013/08/21/business/global/chinese-agency-to-increase-financial-coordination.html.

78. Wei and Davis, "China's Central Bank Prevails in Policy Battles Over Economic Future."

generally attempted to talk down the likelihood of stimulus and refrained from any broad loosening of monetary policy until November 2014.[79]

The events of June 2013 provide an early illustration of several characteristics of the Xi administration's approach to financial reform, and economic policymaking more generally, that have emerged during its first two years. The most obvious is a preference for an opaque, rapid, and personalized approach to economic decisionmaking. The decision to engineer the liquidity shock was taken at the highest levels, implemented by a single agency, and, interview evidence suggests, carried out without significant consultation or coordination with other relevant ministries (let alone with market players). This decisive, one-ministry approach has benefits, but also carries risks, including, as noted in one Xinhua commentary, that of unintended consequences.[80] While the liquidity crunch did help to curtail interbank borrowing, many banks' liquidity needs forced them to aggressively seek deposits through other, equally risky, channels.[81]

A lack of transparency and clear communication was also evident even as the policy was being implemented.[82] Although regulators had warned banks previously to improve their risk management, neither the PBOC nor higher authorities publicly acknowledged that the liquidity shortage was deliberate. Instead, they held that liquidity was sufficient, and urged banks to play their role as market stabilizers. This approach was unorthodox, generated significant resentment, and, at the time, exacerbated market confusion and the stress placed on smaller banks. It also exposed the PBOC to accusations of mismanagement, and, while the lack of transparency did not initially impair the policy's effectiveness, it did once the crisis reached a fever pitch on June 20.[83] At that point, the failure of the PBOC's behind-the-scenes reassurances to restore order illustrates the authorities' limits in managing markets behind the scenes, and suggests that, for a ruling party steeped in secrecy,

---

79. The November 2014 PBOC decision to lower its benchmark interest rate for the first time since 2012 was accompanied by expansion of the floating range for deposit rates. Specifically, the PBOC began allowing banks to offer deposit rates up to 20 percent above its benchmark (previously the ceiling had been 10 percent above benchmark). This represented an important step toward eventual liberalization of deposit rates that partially offset the effect of the cut in the benchmark lending rate. The PBOC would repeat this maneuver in late-February 2015, simultaneously lowering its benchmark rate and raising the deposit rate ceiling to 30 percent above the benchmark. For a translation of the PBOC's statement on the first cut and related actions, see John Liu, Xin Zhou, and Sarah Chen, "China's Central Bank Comments on Interest Rate Cut (Translation)," Bloomberg, November 21, 2014, http://www.bloomberg.com/news/articles/2014-11-21/china-s-central-bank-comments-on-interest-rate-cut-translation-.

80. Zhang Yi and Yao Yujie, "Xinhua Insight: PBOC ends credit crunch, needs to go further," Xinhua, June 26, 2013, http://news.xinhuanet.com/english/indepth/2013-06/26/c_132489308.htm.

81. For example, through the issuance of new, high-yield wealth management products.

82. There is some debate on the clarity of the PBOC's communication prior to the shock, given its earlier warnings to banks to manage their liquidity better. What is clear is that the PBOC's warnings were not effective, whether due to a lack of clarity, credibility, the influence of vested interests, or other factors. Some analysts have also argued that there was a deliberate lack of transparency as part of an effort to preempt opposition. For example, see Rosen and Bao, "China's Interbank Squeeze."

83. As Jiang Jianqing, the head of Industrial and Commercial Bank of China and himself an alternate member of the 18th CCP Central Committee, opined after the shock, "We hope that in the future, policy expectations can be clearer. That would help us understand the overall market situation better and more deeply. . . . If we're going to be of help, we also need policy expectations to be even clearer and more stable."

learning to manage expectations in a modern, mostly market economy remains a work in progress.

Lastly, June provides a useful example of an important, and often overlooked, characteristic of Chinese economic policymaking: its flexibility on details. Despite the Chinese government's well-known penchant for planning and numerical targets, the plans themselves are also notable for their vagueness and rarely prescribe precise means to achieve specified ends. This vagueness, however much it may reflect uncertainty on the part of Chinese policymakers, also provides crucial space for decisionmaking to evolve in light of changing circumstances. In the case of June, it was clear that Beijing was concerned about the pace of credit growth during the first half of 2013, and viewed curtailing financial excesses as an important policy objective. When initial warnings and regulatory measures failed to take effect and, indeed, the problem continued to worsen, a different—arguably riskier—approach emerged. Even as the initial failure speaks to the extent of the challenges in China's financial system, the leadership's flexibility in engineering and authorizing an unorthodox response augurs well for its future effectiveness.

## THE WIDENING OF THE RENMINBI TRADING BAND IN THE FIRST QUARTER OF 2014

In the first quarter of 2014, Beijing took an important step toward the liberalization of its exchange rate by widening the daily RMB trading band. To do so, the PBOC used an unorthodox strategy of first intervening sharply in foreign exchange markets to break entrenched expectations of RMB appreciation against the U.S. dollar. This arrested a sustained inflow of foreign portfolio flows into China and generated two-way fluctuation in the exchange rate: the PBOC's desired conditions for widening the band. The events of the first quarter of 2014 illustrate the evolving domestic politics of China's exchange rate; how different types of external pressure factor into economic decisionmaking; and the incremental, sequenced approach to financial reform preferred by Chinese policymakers.

### *Intervening to Reduce Intervention*

Despite earning only a single mention in the November 2013 Third Plenum Decision, moving toward a more market-determined RMB exchange rate remains a key pillar of Beijing's financial reform agenda. A more market-determined exchange rate system would not only simplify other aspects of Chinese financial reform but also reduce or remove the need for Beijing to continue accumulating foreign reserves. It would also help to eliminate a long-standing, high-profile irritant in U.S.-China relations, and is an important component of Beijing's efforts to internationalize the RMB.

The RMB exchange rate has long been an issue of contest domestically and abroad. For example, responding to the global financial crisis, Beijing decided in July 2008 to peg the RMB to the dollar in order to support growth and economic stability. With China's annual current account surplus approaching 10 percent that year, this decision triggered strong pressure from the United States and others to allow the RMB to appreciate in line with market fundamentals.[84] Chinese officials rejected this pressure, with Premier Wen Jiabao insisting that "a stable yuan is not only good for the Chinese economy, but the world."[85] It was not until June 2010 that the PBOC announced the RMB would be allowed to resume gradual appreciation and enjoy more flexibility moving forward, while warning that it remained "important to avoid any sharp and massive fluctuations of the exchange rate."[86]

China's domestic debate over the value of the RMB has tended to center around MOFCOM and the PBOC jockeying for the support of top leaders. The former, arguing in support of Chinese exporters threatened by the prospect of a stronger currency (mostly in coastal provinces), has long sought to limit the rate of RMB appreciation. The PBOC, focusing on the risks to inflation and financial stability posed by maintaining an undervalued currency, has tended to argue for faster appreciation. Other bureaucratic actors involved in the debate, though to a lesser degree, include the NDRC, which looks at the RMB through the lens of its impact on the structural adjustment of the economy; the Ministry of Industry and Information Technology,[87] which has in the past intervened on behalf of exporters; and MOF, which is responsible for disbursing subsidies to export companies through export tax rebates.[88]

From the start of the Xi administration (and even before), this debate had largely swung in favor of the PBOC viewpoint. Top leadership was increasingly concerned about structural imbalances in the economy and convinced of the need to rebalance toward more consumption-led growth. A stronger RMB would support this process by making imports cheaper. Moreover, as China's foreign exchange reserves had grown into the trillions, they had become more and more expensive to sterilize and maintain. Appreciation would reduce the need for further intervention, both in the foreign exchange markets and to avoid inflationary pressure at home. A more market-based process for determining the exchange rate would also provide an automatic stabilizing mechanism for adjusting to capital inflows and outflows.

Since April 2012, the PBOC had allowed the RMB to fluctuate within a band of ±1 percent around a daily reference rate.[89] This provided policymakers with a means to gauge market sentiment, while still controlling the pace and extent of fluctuations in the RMB's value. Since being introduced in 1994, the band had been widened in stages, and Chinese policymakers had established their intent to continue this process as part of the overall process of RMB liberalization. In April 2013, SAFE Administrator Yi Gang indicated

---

84. Morrison and Labonte, "China's Currency Policy."
85. Li Xiaokun and Cheng Guangjin, "Protectionism, yuan pressure 'unfair': Wen," *China Daily*, December 1, 2009, http://www.chinadaily.com.cn/china/2009-12/01/content_9081886.htm.
86. Morrison and Labonte, "China's Currency Policy."
87. He Xingqiang, "The RMB Exchange Rate: Interest Groups in China's Economic Policy Making," *China Security*, issue 19 (2011), http://ias.cass.cn/en/show_project_ls.asp?id=1569.
88. Wen Jin Yuan, "China's Export Lobbying Groups and the Politics of the Renminbi," CSIS, February 2012, http://csis.org/files/publication/fr12n0102.pdf.
89. The band, set at 0.3 percent in 1994, had been widened over the years as part of a gradual liberalization of the exchange rate, expanding to 0.5 percent in 2007.

that China would widen its trading band "in the near future."[90] Toward the end of that year, both Yi and PBOC Governor Zhou made further statements to this effect, raising expectations that the band would be widened sometime in the first half of 2014.

As of February 2014, the RMB had enjoyed an 18-month run of near-continuous appreciation and, by some estimates, was nearing a "fair value" relative to the U.S. dollar.[91] This had triggered a surge of disguised portfolio inflows into China, which sought to take advantage of the RMB as a "one way bet."[92] These inflows increased domestic liquidity at a time when Beijing was seeking to both rein in excess credit growth and pursue greater financial liberalization. Responding to this, former PBOC deputy governor Hu Xiaolian issued a statement on February 18, in which she joined other officials in expressing concern about the dangers posed by "hot money" flowing into China.[93] The next day, the PBOC began guiding the daily reference rate lower and instructing state-owned banks to purchase dollars, driving the exchange rate sharply downward.[94] On February 26 alone, the RMB fell 0.46 percent against the dollar, its largest single-day fall since 2010.

From mid-February through April, the RMB lost 3.2 percent of its value against the dollar in real terms.[95] This triggered enormous losses for speculators who had bet on the RMB's continued steady appreciation, estimated to be on the order of $5.5 billion.[96] It also introduced two-way fluctuation in the value of the RMB, signaling that it would not be a one-way bet going forward and thereby creating a deterrent against future speculation. This also created the space for the PBOC to fulfill its pledges to widen the RMB trading band. On March 15, during the annual "two meetings" of the NPC and CPPCC[97] where Chinese leaders present the annual government work report and announce the coming year's growth target, the PBOC announced that it would double the RMB trading band to ±2 percent per day.[98]

The PBOC, SAFE, and other government agencies denied that intervention had triggered the depreciation. Governor Zhou and Minister of Finance Lou Jiwei publicly dismissed the RMB's fall as a sign of normal market processes, and SAFE issued a statement to the same

---

90. Natasha Brereton-Fukui and Bob Davis, "China Vows Wider Yuan Movement," *Wall Street Journal*, April 17, 2013, http://www.wsj.com/articles/SB10001424127887323309604578429253732688858.

91. Martin Kessler and Arvind Subramanian, "Is the Renminbi Still Undervalued? Not According to New PPP Estimates," *RealTime Economic Issues Watch*, May 1, 2014, http://blogs.piie.com/realtime/?p=4300.

92. Pete Sweeney, "Hot money distorts China's exports as speculators seek to cash in on yuan, rate reforms," Reuters, December 11, 2013, http://www.reuters.com/article/2013/12/11/us-china-economy-hot-money-idUSBRE9BA0DA20131211.

93. Lingling Wei, "China Allows Wider Currency Fluctuation," *Wall Street Journal*, March 15, 2014, http://www.wsj.com/articles/SB10001424052702303546204579440813396189476.

94. Ibid.

95. Bob Davis, "Yuan Depreciation Is Deeper Than You Think," *Wall Street Journal*, April 18, 2014, http://blogs.wsj.com/chinarealtime/2014/04/18/yuan-depreciation-is-deeper-than-you-think/.

96. Ye Xie and Kyoungwha Kim, "China Burns Speculators as $5.5 Billion Lost on Yuan Bets," Bloomberg, April 1, 2014, http://www.bloomberg.com/news/2014-04-01/china-burns-speculators-as-5-5-billion-lost-on-yuan-bets.html.

97. The NPC and CPPCC both meet in full plenary sessions annually in early March. Referred to as the "two meetings," this is an important event in China's annual political calendar.

98. Josh Noble, "China relaxes controls on exchange rate," *Financial Times*, March 15, 2014, http://www.ft.com/intl/cms/s/0/ea819706-ac37-11e3-b510-00144feab7de.html?siteedition=intl.

effect. "Uncertainty is always present," Zhou remarked to Bloomberg News on February 21; "there's nothing big to worry about."[99] However, the subsequent release of data on China's reserve accumulation during this period revealed that the PBOC had indeed intervened to drive the exchange rate downward. Around the time of the data release, stories in official media would also confirm the PBOC's intervention.[100]

### *Depreciation and Decisionmaking*

It is often noted that the PBOC is not an independent central bank. It is under the supervision of the State Council, which approves all major decisions on monetary policy. The PBOC may voice its views on these issues during State Council meetings (where MOFCOM has equal ability to do the same), and through the monetary policy committee. This advisory committee meets on a quarterly basis, and is composed of representatives from the PBOC, SAFE, the financial regulatory commissions, MOF, the NDRC, an academic expert, and others.[101] Its role is to advise the State Council on the decisions regarding monetary policy.

The widening of the band was a decision of enough significance to warrant discussion by the State Council, though interlocutors gave conflicting reports of the precise process and the level at which consultations took place. Analysts and policymakers interviewed for this report indicated that the PBOC likely received official permission to widen the band well in advance of doing so, and was simply waiting for the right conditions to do so. In other words, while the policy direction was determined at the State Council level (or above), the PBOC was given control over the tactics and timing of its implementation. The decision to widen immediately after intervening to introduce two-way volatility in the market can be a seen as a pragmatic approach to achieving two simultaneous objectives: an incremental step toward greater exchange rate flexibility; and the breaking of entrenched inflation expectations that were encouraging excessive portfolio inflows.

This highlights Chinese financial policymakers' pragmatic, incremental, and evidence-based approach to reform. The last time the PBOC widened the band was in April 2012, during a period of unusual two-way volatility in the RMB's exchange rate against the dollar. In 2014, having committed to a near-term widening of the band in statements following the Third Plenum, the PBOC then acted decisively to break entrenched expectations of appreciation, simultaneously hitting back at speculators and created the conditions for smoothly widening the band. Doing so both enhanced the PBOC's credibility in meeting self-imposed reform deadlines and demonstrated that it was not afraid to discipline the market when it deemed necessary. It also maintained the PBOC's control over the exchange rate: the PBOC-set daily reference rate continues to determine the rate of the RMB's appreciation. The

99. Paul Panckhurst, "China Sees Expansion Outweighing Yuan, Shadow Bank Risk," Bloomberg, February 23, 2014, http://www.bloomberg.com/news/articles/2014-02-23/china-downplays-yuan-banking-risk-as-zhou-sees-7-to-8-growth.

100. "March forex purchases by PBOC behind falling yuan," Xinhua, May 7, 2014, http://news.xinhuanet.com/english/china/2014-05/07/c_133316949.htm.

101. People's Bank of China, "Monetary Policy Committee," http://www.pbc.gov.cn/publish/english/980/index.html.

decision to widen the band was an important step toward a more market-determined exchange rate, but hardly a decisive one.

The PBOC's actions highlight the impact of external factors on Chinese policymaking. As mentioned, large portfolio capital inflows at the start of 2014 complicated the PBOC's management of domestic liquidity and posed a hurdle to widening the RMB trading band. In response, Chinese policymakers devised the unorthodox solution of intervening through state-owned banks. By doing so, the PBOC revealed two things about its decisionmaking. First (and unsurprisingly), it showed the PBOC's keen attention to the movements of international capital markets when making decisions related to monetary policy. Careful, evidence-based policymaking is essential in an environment where stability is of paramount importance. Second, it demonstrated that Beijing was willing to court the almost inevitable ire of the United States and others in order to achieve its domestic objectives.

Finally, the events of the first quarter of 2014 illustrate the evolving domestic politics and debate surrounding China's exchange rate. Following the global financial crisis, the PBOC had to fight in favor of faster RMB appreciation against MOFCOM and others focused on representing interests resistant to structural change in the economy.[102] For a period afterward, it was clear that Chinese leaders understood gradual appreciation of the RMB as supporting the desired shift toward more services- and consumption-led growth. This was a victory for the PBOC, helping to limit its need to intervene in the foreign exchange markets or conduct offsetting sterilization operations, and thereby simplifying the overall task of maintaining financial stability.

Given that the PBOC has long been the strongest bureaucratic advocate in favor of a more market-based exchange rate (which has historically made it an advocate of appreciation), it is unlikely it faced any major opposition in temporarily shifting tactics to encourage depreciation. However, that the RMB subsequently resumed appreciation from late April through the end of 2014 reveals an important shift in China's domestic politics regarding the exchange rate. In the main, China has been pragmatic in managing its exchange rate.[103] At the same time, internal pressure against appreciation was an important factor behind the gradual rate of the RMB's rise and the delay in ending the dollar peg instituted in response to the global financial crisis.[104] That such infighting was not evident in early 2014 and did not appear to influence the RMB's movements through the rest of the year is evidence that the PBOC's view continued to hold sway. It is also evidence that the RMB's nearness to "fair valuation" (alongside China's growing macroeconomic difficulties) has introduced new nuance into the debate. Two-way volatility, while initially artificially induced, now appears likely to sustain itself.

---

102. Nicholas R. Lardy, *Sustaining China's Economic Growth after the Global Financial Crisis* (Washington, DC: Peterson Institute for International Economics, 2012).

103. Arthur R. Kroeber, "New Rules of the Game for China's Renminbi," Brookings Institution, May 14, 2014, http://www.brookings.edu/research/opinions/2014/05/14-new-rules-china-renminbi-kroeber.

104. Freeman and Yuan, *China's Exchange Rate Politics*.

## THE CHINA (SHANGHAI) PILOT FREE-TRADE ZONE (FTZ)

In July 2013, Beijing announced with great fanfare the China (Shanghai) Pilot Free-Trade Zone, with the promise of freer trade, greater financial openness, and fewer government controls in a 29-square-kilometer zone located in China's largest city. More than a year after its debut, reforms implemented in the FTZ have been more incremental than decisive, due in part to disagreements and coordination challenges between the leadership in Beijing, officials in Shanghai, and the ministries tasked with designing the zone's reforms. Limited progress on capital account liberalization, one of the main reforms emphasized in the zone's initial framing, also underscores the leadership's continued risk-averse approach to financial reform.

The evolution of what is so far the highest-profile economic experiment undertaken by the Xi leadership highlights China's persistent internal coordination challenges, as well as other established patterns of Chinese policymaking. These include the importance of external pressure in guiding the overall reform process, and the leadership's continued preference for experimentation and "crossing the river by feeling the stones," even as reforms enter "deeper water." At the same time, the experiment is ongoing—the initial proposed timeline for the zone to meet "international standards" was three years—and any final verdict on its impact remains premature.

### *Initial Stages: "Not a Special Zone or a New Area . . . A New System"*

Shanghai is one of the wealthiest and most developed provinces in China, with long ambitions of becoming a global financial center.[105] It is also a province with deep significance for the Communist Party leadership: seven former Shanghai party secretaries have gone on to membership on the PBSC over the past two decades, and two have served as its head (including Xi Jinping). The choice of Shanghai to host what remains the highest-profile liberalization experiment so far introduced by the Xi administration reflects both of these factors: the relative sophistication of the Shanghai government was critical to piloting the "transformation of government functions" and financial liberalization at the heart of the initiative; and its closeness to Beijing was a key guarantor that Shanghai would stick to the script in implementing a potentially risky reform agenda.

The idea for creating a Shanghai FTZ dates back over a decade, having been first publicly introduced by the then Shanghai party secretary Chen Liangyu in early 2003.[106] Following Chen's 2006 ouster in a major corruption scandal, the idea then lay dormant until 2009, when a proposal for such a zone reached the desk of the then premier Wen Jiabao. Prepared at the behest of one of Shanghai's district governments by the Chinese Association of Productivity Sciences (a Beijing think tank), the plan intrigued Wen enough

105. Cheng Li, "Reclaiming the 'Head of the Dragon': Shanghai as China's Center for International Finance and Shipping," *China Leadership Monitor*, no. 28 (Spring 2009), http://www.hoover.org/sites/default/files/uploads/documents/CLM28CL.pdf.

106. A report by the Shanghai Institute for Productivity on the possibility of a Shanghai FTZ published in the 1990s predates this initiative, but was shelved soon after completion. The 2003 proposal emerged in response to a call from Beijing to improve existing tax-free zones following China's 2001 WTO accession.

for him to rebrand it as a "free-trade park" and order the NDRC to send an inspection team to Shanghai to conduct further study. This proved to be the end of the initiative for the time being: it foundered on opposition from the NDRC and other central ministries. With Premier Wen unwilling or uninterested in committing major political capital to its advancement, the free-trade park quietly failed to materialize.

The revival of the Shanghai FTZ initiative began in early 2013. In January, Shanghai Party Secretary Han Zheng published an article on the importance of reform for Shanghai in a leading party journal, "Seeking Truth," spurring subsequent media reports that Shanghai was developing an FTZ initiative,[107] which was presented to Xi Jinping during the annual NPC meetings in mid-March.[108] Premier Li Keqiang then visited Shanghai later that month,[109] reportedly asking Han and Mayor Yang Xiong whether Shanghai was seeking favorable policies or tough reform (the answer: tough reform).[110] Internal processes to establish the FTZ subsequently began in earnest at both the central and local levels.[111] In early May, the Shanghai municipal government called a meeting to begin drafting a general plan for the FTZ, while later that month MOFCOM began soliciting opinions from "25 relevant ministries" regarding the plan for the zone's establishment.[112]

Between Premier Li's Shanghai visit and the start of these internal processes, another event had taken place that, according to senior Chinese policy advisers, provided a major impetus for the Shanghai experiment. On April 12, 2013, the United States had announced its support for Japan to enter the ongoing TPP negotiations.[113] While Tokyo would not formally join the talks until late July, the de facto addition of the world's third-largest economy—and a major Chinese rival—lent the TPP critical credibility and momentum. It also sparked a dramatic change in China's attitude toward the initiative. Having mostly dismissed the TPP as a form of economic containment prior to Japan's joining,[114] China subsequently adopted a position of cautious interest in the negotiations, and to consider the possibility of eventual Chinese participation in such a high-standard agreement.

---

107. Ying Liqi, "韩正 ：上海要先行先试 走在全国改革开放最前列" [Han Zheng: Shanghai Need to Take Action and Trials to be the Forerunner of China's Economic Reform and Liberalization], January 30, 2013, http://news.sohu.com/20130130/n365044617.shtml.

108. Hu Shuli, "How Shanghai's Free Trade Zone Works," Caixin, January 8, 2014, http://www.chinafile.com/how-shanghais-free-trade-zone-works.

109. "Premier underlines developing scale farming," Xinhua, March 31, 2013, http://www.china.org.cn/china/2013-03/31/content_28408103_2.htm.

110. Lydia Guo, "Shanghai free-trade zone: Low key start, big future," *Financial Times*, October 4, 2013, http://blogs.ft.com/beyond-brics/2013/10/04/shanghai-free-trade-zone-low-key-start-big-future/.

111. Hu Shuli, "How Shanghai's Free Trade Zone Works," Caixin, January 8, 2014, http://www.chinafile.com/how-shanghais-free-trade-zone-works.

112. Ibid.

113. William H. Cooper and Mark E. Manyin, "Japan Joins the Trans-Pacific Partnership: What Are the Implications?" Congressional Research Service, August 13, 2013, https://www.fas.org/sgp/crs/row/R42676.pdf.

114. Joseph Xiaojin Zhang, "News Analysis: May U.S. expand influence in region through TPP?," Xinhua, December 3, 2012, http://news.xinhuanet.com/english/indepth/2012-12/03/c_132016308.htm; "China to study possibility of joining TPP: MOC," Xinhua, May 30, 2013, http://news.xinhuanet.com/english/china/2013-05/30/c_132420541.htm; "China weighs choices on pacific trade pacts: Experts," Xinhua, June 19, 2013, http://usa.chinadaily.com.cn/business/2013-06/19/content_16638291.htm.

Developments gathered pace on both the domestic and international fronts through the following months. On June 28, the Shanghai municipal government submitted its application to establish an FTZ to the State Council, receiving approval from its executive committee less than a week later. Shortly afterward, the annual Strategic and Economic Dialogue commenced in Washington. To the surprise of its U.S. counterparts, the Chinese delegation sought during the dialogue to revive negotiations over a bilateral investment treaty (BIT), stalled since 2010.[115] While the restart of the BIT negotiations was on its face unrelated to the proposed Shanghai experiment, Washington had set two preconditions for their resumption: that China guarantee American companies preestablishment right to national treatment, and that Beijing transition to a negative list approach to regulating FDI. These same reforms would feature at the center of Shanghai's efforts to "transform government functions" and "build the FTZ up to international standards," indicating the leadership's intent to link China's domestic and international economic agendas as part of its reform strategy.[116]

Around this time, unconfirmed reports also began to emerge of ministerial opposition to the Shanghai initiative, similar to that which stifled the "free-trade park" initiative under Wen. On July 15, the *South China Morning Post* broke an exclusive story that Premier Li Keqiang had "lost his temper . . . [and] slammed his fist on the table" in reaction to financial industry regulators' resistance to the FTZ reforms at a closed-door cabinet meeting.[117] Along with reports of a new direct reporting arrangement between the Shanghai municipal government and the premier's office, ostensibly designed to prevent ministerial logjams from impeding the zone's development, this strengthened impressions of the FTZ as the premier's personal initiative—and served as a warning of the challenges ahead.[118]

Notwithstanding these reports, throughout the summer leading up to the FTZ's end-September launch expectations were stoked and duly mounted. Referencing the famous coastal experiment that helped jump-start China's early reforms, articles in the official Chinese press heralded the Shanghai FTZ as "the country's most significant reform push since . . . the Shenzhen Special Economic Zone."[119] The FTZ would allow the leadership to realize "'season two' of China's economic miracle," help China escape the middle-income trap, "get involved in the process of writing global trade rules," and make Shanghai into a

115. U.S. Department of the Treasury, "U.S. Fact Sheet—Economic Track Fifth Meeting of the U.S.-China Strategic and Economic Dialogue," July 12, 2013, http://www.treasury.gov/press-center/press-releases/Pages/jl2011.aspx.

116. "China's Congress discusses Shanghai FTZ," Xinhua, August 26, 2013, http://news.xinhuanet.com/english/china/2013-08/26/c_125251562.htm.

117. George Chen, "Exclusive: Li Keqiang fought strong opposition for Shanghai free-trade zone plan," *South China Morning Post*, July 15, 2013, http://www.scmp.com/news/china/article/1282793/li-fought-strong-opposition-shanghai-free-trade-zone-plan.

118. Shirley Yam, "Leaders bypass ministries on Shanghai free-trade zone," *South China Morning Post*, September 28, 2013, http://www.scmp.com/business/article/1319531/leaders-bypass-ministries-shanghai-free-trade-zone.

119. "News Analysis: Shanghai FTZ outlines roadmap of China's new reform drive," Xinhua, September 29, 2013, http://news.xinhuanet.com/english/indepth/2013-09/29/c_132761883.htm.

"free port" of RMB internalization.[120] Such was the level of excitement that domestic stocks with the word "Shanghai" in their name rose nearly 30 percent from mid-August to mid-September, trading on expectations and enthusiasm alone (the FTZ's general plan had not yet been released).[121] Foreign analysts were somewhat more hesitant in their endorsements, but most saw the leadership's decision to introduce a major economic reform initiative so soon after entering office as at least a strong signal of Beijing's reformist intent.[122]

### *The FTZ in Action: Gnawing Through Hard Bones*

The Shanghai FTZ officially debuted on September 29, 2013, with a first draft of the much-touted negative list released the following day.[123] With expectations so high, many observers predictably reacted with some disappointment. New reports noted with puzzlement the absence of the premier at the opening ceremony, given perceptions of the zone as "his" project.[124] As one Beijing-based interviewee later noted, "This put a damper on the FTZ—if they wanted a bang, they should have at least waited for a vice premier" (the highest-ranking representative from the central government at the ceremony was Minister of Commerce Gao Hucheng). The substance of the reforms also disappointed for their vagueness and perceived lack of ambition. The first draft of the negative list was as restrictive, and arguably more burdensome, than the existing positive list regime. Initial comments from many central government agencies, the PBOC in particular, appeared to stress the importance of caution over the need for bold reforms.[125]

Given the proposed three-year timeline for the FTZ experiment, these negative reactions were at least somewhat premature, reflecting the management of expectations in the lead up to the zone's unveiling more than its actual prospects. After all, there were other clear signs that the FTZ was a serious priority for China's leadership. The Politburo had lent its support in late August, urging the State Council, Shanghai municipal government, "and all related government departments to work together to forge ahead with the program."[126] In late September, the State Council had also made clear its support, and took the unusual additional step of announcing that "should the Shanghai municipal government encounter

---

120. "Shanghai FTZ to further promote China's reform, opening up: Experts," Xinhua, August 24, 2013, http://news.xinhuanet.com/english/china/2013-08/26/c_132662557.htm.

121. Bloomberg, "It's Shanghai or Burst," *South China Morning Post*, September 19, 2013, http://www.scmp.com/business/money/markets-investing/article/1312519/its-shanghai-or-burst.

122. Beina Xu, "What Shanghai's Free Trade Zone Bodes for China," Council on Foreign Relations, October 8, 2013, http://www.cfr.org/china/shanghais-free-trade-zone-bodes-china/p31585.

123. The State Council also released a draft of the FTZ's general plan two days in advance of the zone's opening. The State Council, "国务院关于印发中国（上海）自由贸易试验区总体方案的通知" [The State Council's Notice of Establishing the China (Shanghai) Pilot Free-Trade Zone], September 27, 2013, http://www.gov.cn/zwgk/2013-09/27/content_2496147.htm.

124. Andrew Browne, "Questions Arise about Beijing's Support for Free-Trade Zone: Premier Li Keqiang Doesn't Attend Launch of Shanghai Free-Trade Zone," *Wall Street Journal*, October 7, 2013, http://online.wsj.com/news/articles/SB10001424052702304626104579121011334166376.

125. Not unjustifiably, given the potential for improperly sequenced financial liberalization to create instability. See Nicholas Borst, "The Shanghai Free Trade Zone: Ring-Fencing Financial Liberalization," *China Economic Watch*, September 30, 2013, http://blogs.piie.com/china/?p=3272.

126. "China's central authorities back Shanghai FTZ," Xinhua, August 27, 2013, http://news.xinhuanet.com/english/china/2013-08/27/c_132668049.htm.

any major problem, it should be promptly reported to the State Council"—in effect confirming that Shanghai would have a direct line to the premier's office.[127] This effort to empower the Shanghai government reflected the leadership's concern that bureaucratic stalling, similar to that which had undermined the earlier "free-trade park" proposal, could scuttle the FTZ initiative. By making clear that Shanghai, with its direct stake in seeing the zone succeed, enjoyed direct access to top leaders, it was hoped this might be avoided.[128]

The remainder of 2013 saw a flurry of zone-related activity. By end-December, a dozen ministries, including the four ministry-level financial regulators, had released regulations related to the zone's implementation.[129] Nearly 3,500 companies,[130] including 228 foreign-invested enterprises and 12 foreign banks, had used the newly created FTZ administration to register in the zone.[131] A dedicated Financial Work Coordination Group, chaired by Shanghai Executive Vice Mayor Tu Guangshao, had been established to advance the FTZ's financial reform agenda. The zone had also received a high-profile endorsement from the November Third Plenum, with the Decision describing it as "a major measure to move reform and opening under new circumstances." Coming in a document designed to set the agenda for a decade of reforms, this reference was particularly meaningful and a further demonstration of the leadership's support.

Despite this extensive surface-level activity, however, it was unclear whether implementation of any truly significant reforms was under way. Many measures, such as those put forward by the PBOC, seemed to focus less on market-based reform and more on preventing the effects of any Shanghai initiatives from spilling over into the rest of China.[132] These concerns would deepen through the first half of 2014. Foreign companies in particular began to complain about a lack of meaningful reforms,[133] and representatives of a number of those invested in the zone privately acknowledged that their decision had been more politically than commercially motivated. In off-the-record conversations, senior Shanghai policy advisers described growing tension between the Shanghai authorities, which were seeking a faster pace of reform, and the more cautious approach preferred by central government agencies. A debate was also ongoing as to the priorities of the zone: whether its first focus

---

127. Yam, "Leaders bypass ministries on Shanghai free-trade zone."

128. The institutional setup for the FTZ's implementation also reflected this concern. Prior to its opening, the State Council established two leading groups in Beijing and Shanghai. The higher-level Beijing body brought together representatives from roughly 20 agencies under the joint leadership of the Shanghai municipal government, MOFCOM, and the NDRC. The Shanghai-level group was similarly structured. Thus, while the NDRC and MOFCOM would take leadership in the actual design of the FTZ plan, Shanghai, with its direct line to the State Council, would have unusual sway in ensuring its implementation.

129. MOFCOM, the PBOC, MIIT, MOF, the Ministry of Culture, the Ministry of Transport, the General Administration of Customs, State Administration of Taxation, State Administration of Industry and Commerce, General Administration of Quality Supervision, Inspection, and Quarantine, CBRC, CSRC, and CIRC.

130. Sina Finance, "上海自贸区2013年新设企业3405户" [The Addition of 3405 Companies in Shanghai FTZ in 2013], January 6, 2014, http://finance.sina.com.cn/stock/t/20140106/172717859094.shtml.

131. Sina News, "上海自贸区 ：改革红利初现" [Shanghai FTZ: The Emerging Benefits of the Reform], January 9, 2014, http://news.sina.com.cn/c/2014-01-09/162529199303.shtml.

132. Nicholas Borst, "The Shanghai Free Trade Zone's Financial Firewall," *China Economic Watch*, December 6, 2013, http://blogs.piie.com/china/?p=3593.

133. Michelle Chen, "Reform paralysis, slow progress cloud Shanghai free trade zone project," Reuters, September 15, 2014, http://www.reuters.com/article/2014/09/14/china-shanghai-ftz-idUSL3N0RB1JR20140914.

should be on promoting financial and capital account liberalization (and the strengthening of Shanghai as a financial center), or the "transformation of government functions" and other measures to strengthen the "real economy," such as by eliminating registered capital requirements, shifting from an approval to a registration system for foreign investment, and establishing a "one-stop shop" registration process for new companies.

During his first visit to the zone in May 2014, President Xi sharpened rather than allayed these concerns, deepening the sense of a contradiction between the FTZ's grand purported purpose and the realities on the ground. In remarks reported by CCTV, he stressed that management of the FTZ would require a combination of "structural reform and the exploration of new methods, while controlling risks and gradually making improvements."[134] Although consistent with China's traditional pattern of achieving reform through "crossing the river by feeling the stones," this call for caution sat uncomfortably alongside leaders' earlier exhortations on the need to act decisively in moving through the "deeper waters" of reform. A *China Daily* article published shortly after Xi's visit neatly captured the apparent contradictions in his remarks: "Few experiments can shun risks. But some must. President Xi Jinping . . . again urged [Shanghai] to push the envelope in exploring a transplantable path for financial reform . . . and stressed risk prevention as the baseline for reform."[135]

In an unusual rambling critique, this same article went on to launch criticisms at many of the actors involved in establishing the FTZ. Shanghai's failure to "take the ox's nose" in steering reforms had left enterprises registered in the zone "disappointed with the slow progress." Stalled financial reform was due to opposition from SOEs, banks, and corrupt officials "seeking illegal profits from the power-money trade." Coordination was hindered, according to an official from the FTZ administration quoted in the piece, by the fact that the overlapping responsibilities of central ministries meant that "almost every important reform policies we made is related to more than two central government departments." Even Xi earned some criticism: while "[his] vigilance to the risks of financial reform is justifiable . . . he needs to give more support to help Shanghai coordinate interests and actions of different ministries . . . or, an experimental field will only become a showcase."[136]

While far from representing any official or systematic assessment of the zone's progress, this strange polemic is revealing of many of the issues that were in fact hindering the zone's development: an unclear mandate; a fragmented bureaucratic apparatus, lacking any functional coordination mechanism; uneven capacity for implementing reforms within the bureaucracy; and an apparent absence of sustained, high-level attention. In interviews conducted in July 2014, several interlocutors also noted that, while many Shanghai bureaus (and the financial services office in particular) were enthusiastic about faster

134. Zhang Jianfeng, "Chinese president urges Shanghai stronger competitiveness," Xinhua, May 24, 2014, http://english.cntv.cn/2014/05/24/ARTI1400937821852811.shtml.

135. Li Yang, "Shanghai FTZ needs neat, stable reforms to make it," *China Daily USA*, June 6, 2014, http://usa.chinadaily.com.cn/epaper/2014-06/06/content_17568119.htm.

136. Ibid.

reforms in the zone, the main financial regulators—the PBOC, CBRC, CSRC, and CIRC—were less interested, if not outright opposed. When asked about one of the other major zone reforms, the negative list, one senior government-affiliated researcher said simply, "Expectations are too high," citing the sheer number of agencies involved in the list's compilation as reason enough to justify its excessive length. That this was seen as the case in spite of the clear and deliberate enlistment of external pressure as a lever for reform says much about the strength of bureaucratic intransigence and domestic interests.

### *The Shanghai FTZ: Harbinger or Red Herring?*

As a result, and despite some official rhetoric to the contrary, at the one-year anniversary of the Shanghai FTZ's opening, the *Financial Times* summarized the mood surrounding the experiment as one of palpable disappointment, "with scant progress on loosening capital controls or liberalizing interest rates."[137]

A raft of reforms announced earlier in the year, including a new system of free-trade accounts, liberalization of interest rates on corporations' foreign currency deposits, and the elimination of registered capital requirements, while directionally positive, had failed to stem an emerging consensus that the FTZ experiment was floundering. Even MOFCOM's revised version of the negative list, released in July 2014 with a "27 percent reduction in listed items," was roundly panned. As analysts—and the U.S. Treasury[138]—quickly noted, the reduction mainly reflected the elimination of redundancies in the original list rather than any major new opening.[139] Adding to Shanghai's troubles, Dai Haibo, the FTZ administration's executive deputy director for daily operations, was suspended for suspected disciplinary violations in mid-September.[140]

The full and final fate of the Shanghai FTZ is not clear. The trial was initially slated for three years, and it still has some support in Zhongnanhai, as illustrated by Premier Li's one-year anniversary visit to the zone[141] and President Xi's comments on the zone at the end of October in a meeting of the CDRLSG.[142] In September 2014, the PBOC promised that

---

137. Gabriel Wildau, "Shanghai free-trade zone struggles to live up to its hype," *Financial Times*, September 2, 2014, http://www.ft.com/intl/cms/s/0/b6985580-324f-11e4-b929-00144feabdc0.html#axzz3CY6nqGEL; Shen Hong, "One Year On, Shanghai Free-Trade Zone Disappoints," *Wall Street Journal*, September 28, 2014, http://www.wsj.com/articles/one-year-on-shanghai-free-trade-zone-disappoints-1411928668.

138. "Lew says China update of Shanghai FTZ list contains no major U.S. benefits," *Inside U.S. Trade*, July 1, 2014, https://www.uschina.org/media/inthenews/lew-says-china-update-shanghai-ftz-list-contains-no-major-us-benefits.

139. Lu Jianxin and John Ruwitch, "Shanghai trade zone cuts FDI restrictions, but avoids significant changes," Reuters, July 1, 2014, http://www.reuters.com/article/2014/07/01/china-ftz-negativelist-idUSL4N0PC2LY20140701.

140. "Head of Shanghai's free-trade zone, Dai Haibo, to step down amid graft probe," *South China Morning Post*, September 15, 2014, http://www.scmp.com/news/china/article/1592689/head-shanghais-free-trade-zone-dai-haibo-step-down-amid-graft-probe.

141. "Premier urges more Shanghai FTZ innovation," Xinhua, September 9, 2014, http://www.globaltimes.cn/content/882397.shtml.

142. At the meeting, Xi compared the experience gained through the FTZ to "seeds cultivated in an experimental plot," and promised that China would copy the practices piloted in Shanghai in other places "as soon as possible." This presaged the December approval of the three additional FTZs discussed below. "Xi says China to

financial reform would move faster,[143] and the zone was subsequently expanded in January 2015 to include the central Lujiazui financial district, which will increase the impact of future financial reforms.[144] Even if these are not forthcoming, Shanghai Party Secretary Han Zheng has argued that "the core reform was to transform the government's role,"[145] meaning that an excessive focus on finance or the treatment of foreign enterprises could perhaps be missing the main thrust of the effort (though this does not explain the continued emphasis on capital account opening in official statements).[146]

More likely, however, it appears that the leadership is changing its approach and Shanghai is losing some of its initial prominence. After having denied applications from other provinces to establish their own zones for over a year, in December 2014 the State Council approved the establishment of new zones in three additional provinces.[147] "Following the success of the pilot free-trade zone in Shanghai," the official statement said, "new parks will be opened in Tianjin, Guangdong and Fujian."[148] Coming from a party famous for never officially acknowledging mistakes, this may be a tacit admission of the zone's underperformance to date.

The experiment of the Shanghai FTZ exhibits many traditional characteristics of Chinese economic policymaking, as discussed in Chapter 4 above: persistent coordination challenges within the bureaucracy; a preference for a cautious and incremental approach to liberalization (particularly in finance); the continued challenge of negotiating the gap between the center and the localities; and the use of external pressure and international standards to provide organizing principles for reform.

This last point bears particular attention in understanding an experiment such as the Shanghai FTZ. While China's initial coastal opening to FDI may have been in part about preferential policies to attract foreign investors, the current leadership has explicitly rejected such "favorable policies" in the Shanghai zone. At least conceptually, the primary focus of the zone is not to improve the operating environment for foreign investors, but to improve China's overall business environment and economic outlook through reforms to its administration system. A narrow focus on the demands of foreign companies—and

---

found more FTZs following Shanghai's example," Xinhua, October 27, 2014, http://news.xinhuanet.com/english/china/2014-10/27/c_133746159.htm.

143. "Financial reform to speed up in Shanghai FTZ," Xinhua, September 29, 2014, http://usa.chinadaily.com.cn/business/2014-09/29/content_18683829.htm.

144. Li Yang, "Shanghai FTZ heft quadruples," *China Daily USA*, January 9, 2015, http://usa.chinadaily.com.cn/epaper/2015-01/09/content_19281568.htm.

145. Hu Shuli, "How Shanghai's Free Trade Zone Works," Caixin, January 8, 2014, http://www.chinafile.com/how-shanghais-free-trade-zone-works.

146. "Shanghai to speed up FTZ reforms: Mayor," Xinhua, November 2, 2014, http://news.xinhuanet.com/english/china/2014-11/02/c_133760807.htm.

147. Jamil Anderlini, "New China free trade zones to lift growth," *Financial Times*, December 14, 2014, http://www.ft.com/intl/cms/s/0/dfac8e5e-834f-11e4-9a9a-00144feabdc0.html.

148. These zones will replicate many of the administrative reforms first piloted in the Shanghai FTZ, but each will seek to pilot specialized reforms suited to local conditions and available capacity (just as Shanghai was intended to specialize in promoting financial reform).

their dissatisfaction with zone's progress—can thus be misleading, even as Beijing's apparent disinterest in addressing many of their concerns is itself revealing.

The zone also highlights the difficult challenge facing Chinese officials as they attempt to "let market forces play a decisive role," while remaining proactive in risk prevention. For example, the Chinese administration system has long relied on cumbersome up-front approval processes, but maintained little capacity for follow-up supervision. The reforms under way in the Shanghai FTZ are in large part about reversing this emphasis: lowering barriers to entry and activity, while raising the standards for supervision. Making this system work will require a significant retooling of China's governance apparatus and mindset, one that will be essential to allowing the market a "decisive role" in resource allocation. It is important to recognize that the goal to "transform government functions" is not the empty talk it might seem to Western ears.

At the same time, it would be a mistake to simply write off the limited progress made so far on capital account liberalization as observers misreading Beijing's intentions en masse. The initial framing of the Shanghai experiment put finance front and center on the reform agenda along with administrative reform, and most observers agree that progress on the former has been disappointing. This frustration is not by design. To some degree, it is likely that China's leaders initially oversold the zone, and have since had to roll back their ambitions in light of the difficulties so far encountered. For all Beijing's (real and perceived) penchant for planning, China's leaders are fallible, time-pressed individuals making policy in the context of incomplete information. Their extreme emphasis on maintaining stability makes them hyperaware of the need to adapt policy to changing circumstances, even as their political culture makes public backpedaling difficult.

# The Xi Administration's Approach to Financial Reform

## POLICYMAKING PATTERNS

As the above cases suggest, the Xi administration's approach to financial reform demonstrates both important aspects of continuity with earlier periods and its own distinct characteristics. Perhaps the most distinct characteristic of the Xi leadership's approach to financial reform is a decisive, centralized style of decisionmaking. When a specific, short-term problem is identified, a decisive deployment of specific countermeasures follows. In two of the three cases, this approach proved largely successful in achieving policy objectives. However, as the development of the Shanghai FTZ shows, when the goals of reform are less explicit, the reform requires implementation over a longer time frame, and there is a broader range of actors involved, achieving decisive outcomes has proven more challenging. This suggests that successful implementation in finance and other areas of reform will require the leadership to employ strategies beyond those demonstrated in these case studies.

In other ways, the approach of the Xi leadership has been in keeping with established patterns of Chinese economic policymaking. For example, achieving coordination between Chinese ministries clearly remains a major challenge, and one not easily solved by top leadership's sweeping policy pronouncements. While such pronouncements and the promise to "give the market a decisive role" have set the tone for policies to be implemented, achieving concrete outcomes and effective coordination will additionally require top leaders to take ownership of initiatives and supply the close supervision and clear directives needed to drive processes forward. Even if leaders do take a more hands-on approach, the Shanghai experience shows that there remain important capacity and mindset gaps for designing and implementing more market-based reforms (let alone administering the resulting system) at the local level. These will inevitably take time to address.

Alternatively, leaders may attempt to sidestep coordination altogether, as they did in June 2013 and the first quarter of 2014, empowering one ministry to act decisively to achieve a narrow objective. However, this tactic is not universally applicable; some mechanism for achieving coordination will ultimately be necessary, and such a mechanism is not yet evident. For example, reports suggest the PBOC-led financial regulatory coordinating body established in August 2013 (following the June shock) has been hobbled by interministerial conflict.[149] This is the same problem that frustrated earlier attempts to establish such a regulatory coordinating mechanism, and more general attempts to achieve effective coordination between state agencies of equal formal rank. Coordination also clearly remains a challenge between the central and local governments: even in Shanghai, despite its leaders' close ties to Zhongnanhai and Xi's own experience as its party secretary, this has proven difficult.

A continued preference for experimentation remains evident in financial reform, albeit of an unusually cautious and incremental kind. In the case of the Shanghai FTZ, this "incremental" approach is due at least in part to coordination challenges and other factors discussed earlier. However, it also likely reflects another characteristic of Chinese policymakers' tactics in financial reform more generally: a careful attention to sequencing, widely accepted as central to avoiding instability. This is evident in Beijing's approach to interest rate liberalization, where, among other reforms, deposit insurance has been stressed as an essential prerequisite to full liberalization. It is also the case in exchange rate and capital account reform, where the widening of the RMB trading band and the creation of the Hong Kong–Shanghai stock exchange connection, respectively, represent incremental advancements rather than dramatic leaps toward the eventual (stated) goal of full liberalization.

As is evident in the Shanghai case, the current leadership is also drawing from the tried-and-true playbook of wielding external pressure to drive reform. However, the relatively lackluster progress thus far serves as an important reminder that external pressure alone cannot drive reform; it must be wielded. For example, China's WTO

---

149. Jamil Anderlini, "China bank regulators caught in turf war," *Financial Times*, April 9, 2014, http://www.ft.com/intl/cms/s/0/0eb56cf4-bfc7-11e3-b6e8-00144feabdc0.html?siteedition=intl.

accession was closely overseen by the premier with direct investment in the process, guided and coordinated by the state councilor directly reporting to the premier, and coordinated by two major ministries in close cooperation with the State Council general office.[150] No such approach to the BIT negotiations, or to financial reform, is so far evident, nor is an organizing principle as comprehensive as the WTO accession process necessarily available. In contrast to external *pressure*, however, external *forces*, particularly from financial markets, clearly constrain the options available to Chinese policymakers and influence their policy choices, as demonstrated by June 2013 and the widening of the RMB trading band (as well as China's challenges in dealing with capital outflows in the first quarter of 2015).[151]

## LOOKING AHEAD

The Xi administration has emphasized financial reform as a key element of its overall reform agenda, and it has been an important priority in the administration's first two years. Top leaders and key bureaucrats have repeatedly emphasized its importance in public speeches[152] and major meetings,[153] and maintained that major progress is on the way.[154] Already, incremental progress has been made on all three key areas emphasized in this chapter and by China's leaders: interest rate, exchange rate, and capital account liberalization. Among other reforms, draft rules for deposit insurance were introduced in late 2014, with expected implementation this year, and the RMB's daily trading band was widened. The Hong Kong–Shanghai Stock Connect was announced, marking an important step toward greater capital account liberalization, and authorities have pledged to accelerate financial reforms in the Shanghai FTZ. The continued growth of the shadow-banking sector and Beijing's recent endorsement of Internet finance companies have strengthened competition for deposits within the financial system.

At the same time, it is clear that financial reform has not been the Xi administration's number-one priority since taking office. Other issues, such as the anticorruption campaign and fiscal reform, have taken center stage instead. This may reflect continued uncertainty about how to give the market a "decisive role" in capital allocation without triggering some form of financial instability (and while maintaining party control). It is also possible that China's leaders see anticorruption, fiscal, and SOE reform as prerequisites (or at least necessary complements) for advancing more dramatic, market-oriented financial reforms.

---

150. Yong Wang, "China's Stakes in WTO Accession: The Internal Decision-making Process," in *China's WTO Accession: National and International Perspectives*, ed. Heike Holbig and Robert Ash (London: RoutledgeCurzon, 2002).

151. Fitch Ratings, "China's RRR Cut Less of an Easing Than It Appears," *Fitch Wire*, February 5, 2015, https://www.fitchratings.com/gws/en/fitchwire/fitchwirearticle/China%27s-RRR-Cut?pr_id=979217.

152. For example, Li Keqiang, "Chinese Premier Li Keqiang's speech at Davos 2015" (speech at World Economic Forum, Davos, January 23, 2015), https://agenda.weforum.org/2015/01/chinese-premier-li-keqiangs-speech-at-davos-2015/.

153. "Spotlight: China's continuous reforms, development to boost global economic recovery," Xinhua, December 11, 2014, http://news.xinhuanet.com/english/indepth/2014-12/11/c_133848741.htm.

154. Bob Davis, "China Central Bank Said Committed to Rate Reform," *Wall Street Journal*, July 10, 2014, http://www.wsj.com/articles/pbocs-zhou-still-committed-to-interest-rate-liberalization-in-two-years-1404970714.

This would indicate that Beijing has assessed the risks in the financial system remain manageable at present, and a gradual, sequenced approach is preferable to chancing instability through premature liberalization. During the last major round of economic reforms in China, Zhu Rongji used a similar approach, pursuing financial reform at the same time as he pushed forward a massive campaign to downsize the public sector. This was needed to break up problematic linkages between Chinese banks and uncompetitive SOEs that had led to the NPL buildup in the first place.

There are risks should the Xi administration delay decisive financial reform too long. The McKinsey Global Institute has estimated that China's overall debt-to-GDP ratio reached 282 percent as of mid-2014, accounting for more than a third of postcrisis debt growth in the entire global economy.[155] Even under what it views as favorable assumptions, Goldman Sachs has estimated it would take half a decade of slowing credit growth for this ratio to stabilize.[156] Given the complexity, opacity, interconnectedness, and sheer size of China's financial system, the risk of financial instability—perhaps stemming from a deeper-than-expected property market downturn—cannot be fully discounted.

However, it is not likely that China will experience a full-blown financial crisis in the near term. It has limited external vulnerabilities, and the banking sector is relatively healthy.[157] The IMF has assessed that, even taking into account the rapid growth of local government debt in recent years, the Chinese government has policy tools adequate to avoiding a sharp slowdown.[158] These include a large pool of domestic savings, significant public-sector assets, and low public debt levels. Moreover, China's financial technocrats—in particular, Governor Zhou—are talented reformers of long experience and appear to enjoy the confidence of top leaders.

On balance, it is likely that China will muddle through on financial reform and make some incremental progress. However, the process will almost certainly generate some surprises along the way and may take significantly longer than initially expected.[159] The Chinese financial system is orders of magnitude more complex than during the last major round of reforms, which required the better part of a decade to complete. This magnifies the challenge of advancing reform without upsetting stability. Indeed, in the Third Plenum Decision and elsewhere,[160] top leaders have illustrated that they have a vision for financial reform and a market-based system for capital allocation, even as their actions have demonstrated concern over how to realize this roadmap. For example, the PBOC's attempts to use

155. Pedro Nicolaci da Costa, "China's Total Debt Load Equals 282% of GDP, Raising Economic Risks," *Wall Street Journal*, February 4, 2015, http://blogs.wsj.com/economics/2015/02/04/chinas-total-debt-load-equals-282-of-gdp-raising-its-economic-risks/.

156. David Keohane, "ICYMI, China's credit buildup was pretty damn fast," *Financial Times*, January 26, 2016, http://ftalphaville.ft.com/2015/01/26/2100092/icymi-chinas-credit-buildup-was-pretty-damn-fast/.

157. Huang and Bosler, *China's Debt Dilemma*.

158. IMF, "People's Republic of China: 2012 Article IV Consultation," IMF Country Report No. 12/195, July, 2012, https://www.imf.org/external/pubs/ft/scr/2012/cr12195.pdf.

159. Gabriel Wildau, "China slowdown threatens timetable for financial reform," *Financial Times*, September 28, 2014, http://www.ft.com/intl/cms/s/0/fe7e75b6-43c3-11e4-baa7-00144feabdc0.html.

160. Xiaochuan, "Road map for financial reform."

targeted interventions throughout 2014 to encourage lending to priority sectors (rather than relying on more market-based tools) is a clear message that financial policymakers do not yet trust China's financial system to allocate credit in a manner consistent with their objectives without guidance.[161] This was likely the right policy at the time, but also underscores the challenges that Beijing will face in letting go and ceding the market a decisive role—and the risks it sees in doing so.

161. Gabriel Wildau, "Chinese monetary policy undergoes big shift," *Financial Times*, February 11, 2015, http://www.ft.com/intl/cms/s/0/baee0b5c-b1b1-11e4-8396-00144feab7de.html; Fitch Ratings, "China's RRR Cut Less of an Easing than It Appears."

# 6 Assessing Policymaking under Xi Jinping

## Centralized Economic Decisionmaking

Most analysts of Chinese leadership now accept that Xi Jinping is the most powerful Chinese leader since Deng Xiaoping. A few have even argued that Xi is the most powerful man to occupy Zhongnanhai since Mao Zedong.[1] Whatever the precise extent of Xi's power and whichever comparison is more exactly appropriate, it should come as no surprise that a leader of such widely acknowledged potency has significantly centralized economic decisionmaking and placed a renewed emphasis on the "top-level design" of reform. This has resulted in a much more rapid, opaque, and personalized style of economic decisionmaking under Xi than was evident under his immediate predecessors.

Given that the Hu-Wen leadership was plagued by unusual indecisiveness, this comparison perhaps sets the bar too low. Post-Mao, every generation of Chinese leaders has emphasized the need for consensus-based decisionmaking, but this emphasis reached its apex under Hu and Wen, to the point where it undermined the effectiveness of their leadership.[2] Like Zhu Rongji, the Hu-Wen leadership relied on the state bureaucracy to play the central role in economic policymaking, but proved less effective in managing it. Hu and Wen also struggled to address unintended negative consequences of the decentralization that had begun after Deng's Southern Tour and significantly enhanced the power of the provinces in economic policymaking. Ex post facto assessments of their approach largely agree that it contributed to the stagnation of reform during their tenure and the deepening of China's structural economic problems.

Clearly Xi shares this assessment, and has moved to ensure these problems do not recur under his leadership. Using the CDRLSG and the CFELSG, he has in effect sidestepped the state apparatus and used party channels to create a "counterbureaucracy" for coordinating his reform agenda and "strengthening top-level design." The three adjectives used above to describe Xi's economic decisionmaking style—rapid, opaque, and personalized—follow in

1. Michael Forsythe, "Q. and A.: Roderick MacFarquhar on Xi Jinping's High-Risk Campaign to Save the Communist Party," *New York Times*, January 30, 2015, http://sinosphere.blogs.nytimes.com/2015/01/30/q-and-a-roderick-macfarquhar-on-xi-jinpings-high-risk-campaign-to-save-the-communist-party/.
2. Christopher K. Johnson, "Beijing's Cracked Consensus," *Foreign Affairs*, April 18, 2012, http://www.foreignaffairs.com/articles/137413/christopher-k-johnson/beijings-cracked-consensus.

part from this tactical shift in the center of economic policymaking toward these high-level party institutions, and in part stem from Xi's characteristics as a leader.

By its nature, the party is a more opaque and personalized institution than the formal bureaucracy of the state, particularly at the highest levels. While there has been an unprecedented level of transparency surrounding the membership and agendas of the CDRLSG and CFELSG—even including the partial televising of meetings—their internal workings remain little understood by all but a few high party officials. However, it is clear that these institutions, along with his own keen grasp of party doctrine, have helped Xi to make an unusually fast start in putting forward his economic reform agenda (as well as policy priorities in other areas such as foreign affairs).

Xi's own personal political style reinforces these trends toward rapidity, opacity, and the personalization of economic decisionmaking. His experiences, first as the privileged son of one of the Communist Party regime's founding fathers and later as a victim of the Cultural Revolution, provided him eloquent early instruction in party language, politics, and process. As CSIS scholar Christopher Johnson has phrased it, this background has enabled Xi "to skillfully play to all of the tones in the CCP's ideological register."[3] He relies heavily on centralized control over the varied tools of the party apparatus, from personnel and propaganda to anticorruption and mass-line campaigns, to advance his political agenda, and uses the extent of his arsenal and unpredictability in its employment to keep opponents off-balance.

These trends have reduced the already-limited transparency and predictability of Chinese economic policymaking and disrupted established top-level decisionmaking patterns. The conversation on economic decisions has been elevated and, as a consequence, to a certain degree narrowed.[4] Ministries in key areas headed by trusted technocrats, such as Governor Zhou of the PBOC and MOF's Lou Jiwei, have been empowered, though not through any formal institutional mechanism. Fewer ministries, and fewer officials beyond the top levels, are involved in deciding policy direction, leading both to more rapid decisionmaking and to more decisive action, but also raising the risk of unintended consequences. While centrally controlled economic levers, such as fiscal revenue, financial conditions, and the anticorruption campaign, provide a powerful arsenal for shaping the environment in which officials and economic actors make decisions, they are not without limits. The increased personalization of policymaking in the context of such a broad reform agenda also raises questions as to whether the top leadership, and Xi in particular, will have the bandwidth needed to supervise its implementation—and whether or not trusted implementers, such as Liu He, have enough personal clout to drive top-down change through the system.

---

3. Christopher K. Johnson, *Decoding China's Emerging "Great Power" Strategy in Asia* (Washington, DC: CSIS, June 2014), http://csis.org/files/publication/140603_Johnson_DecodingChinasEmerging_WEB.pdf.

4. The full CFELSG has 26 full members, not all of whom are involved in economic policymaking. This is a larger number than were involved in the plenum drafting body. See Appendix II for a full roster.

Regardless of these challenges, it is clear that Xi is determined to reverse the trends in decisionmaking that handicapped his predecessors, and to ensure more "top-level design" of economic policy. Given the record of the Hu-Wen administration on economic reform, this can only be a good thing, even as it reduces the transparency of decisionmaking. Strategic ambiguity, alongside more rapid decisionmaking, may help Xi to keep opponents of his reforms off-balance and his agenda moving forward. From a substantive perspective, successful top-level design could have enormous positive effects, from promoting more consistent national standards and regulations and limiting local protectionism to encouraging more rational patterns of infrastructure investment and restructuring of regional economies. As an overall trend, this should be read as a net—though not unqualified—positive for China's economic reform prospects.

# Fragmented Policy Implementation

This narrative of new decisiveness only extends so far beyond Zhongnanhai and the top levels of economic decisionmaking. In many respects, the mountains remain high, and the emperor, while powerful, far away. Xi has sidestepped the official bureaucracy in much of top-level decisionmaking, but he remains reliant on it for technical expertise in implementing reform. He has built new channels within the party in an effort make local officials more accountable—and better incentivized—to implement reform, but he has not made new officials.[5] Those in office are the same who flourished for decades under the old "growth first" model of governance. As a result of these and other enduring factors, down to the vast and rugged geography of China itself, the implementation of reform has been, in many ways, uncoordinated and uncertain—as well as unenthusiastic.

Deng Xiaoping was not an economic genius; he was an extremely canny politician. His enduring brilliance was in harnessing positive incentives to build a durable coalition across Chinese society in favor of growth, and reform as a means to achieve it. This meant that, for the most part, bottom-up innovations in policy complemented, and even sometimes inspired, top-down reform initiatives. Today's more pluralized political economy has no such comparable unifying objective. Although present reforms are, in the aggregate, designed to ensure the continued and more sustainable expansion of the economic pie, in their details they represent a major reshuffling of winners and losers across different sectors of the economy and across society. Local bureaucrats and party officials, for example, are set to lose many of their most cherished tools for generating wealth and dispensing patronage if the current reforms go forward.

This helps to explain why implementation of economic reform has so far been unenthusiastic: many measures, such as Premier Li's campaign to reduce excess approval measures, cut hard against vested interests. Local leaders in particular have gone from having among the most privileged, empowered, and influential positions in government, to being

5. The authors would like to thank Kenneth Lieberthal for highlighting this point in several conversations.

squeezed from all sides. Below them, Internet-enabled citizens armed with mobile-phone cameras are watching for signs of graft or bad behavior. From above, they face more varied and difficult-to-accomplish targets, as well as stricter discipline and strengthened scrutiny. Xi himself has warned that party members must "align themselves with the [Central Committee] in deed and thought, at all times and in any situation."[6] Meanwhile, Beijing's efforts to more closely manage the process of reform and restrain the growth of local debt are reducing local leaders' autonomy and cutting off old sources of revenue before new ones have been made clear.[7] This shift has sharpened tensions between the center and the localities and, along with the anti-corruption campaign (discussed below), had the unintended consequence of producing near-paralysis in local decisionmaking.

Implementation has also been uncoordinated, in part as a side effect of Xi's decisionmaking style, as discussed above. By using officials from the CFELSG as a "kitchen cabinet" for drafting the Third Plenum resolution, Xi largely bypassed the ministries in developing a reform agenda they would bear the burden of implementing and enforcing. This likely led to some significant disgruntlement within the state bureaucracy. Moreover, by shifting the center of economic policy coordination into party channels and away from the state, Xi has disrupted established patterns of coordination and communication that, however clogged they may have been, will take time to reorient to the new decisionmaking structure.[8] In the meantime, China's traditional coordination challenges have persisted and in some respects been amplified, with even high-ranking officials in Beijing often unaware of policy direction in their area of responsibility.

Implementation of reform has also been uncertain. This is due in part to another hallmark Xi initiative: the anticorruption campaign, which has cast a chill over the Chinese political system with its unexpected extent and ferocity.[9] Such a clear sign of unrest at the apex of China's political hierarchy as the arrest of a former PBSC member, coupled with the newly enhanced threat of anticorruption probes into bureaucrats and local officials alike, have undermined Xi's calls for "activeness and bold efforts" in implementing market-oriented reforms.[10] While the campaign has undoubtedly helped disincentivize many forms of corruption, it has also created a climate of fear that has strengthened the bureaucracy and local officaldom's "wait and see" bias with regard to many market-based reforms.

---

6. "Xi stresses Party discipline, rules," Xinhua, January 13, 2015, http://news.xinhuanet.com/english/china/2015-01/13/c_133916942.htm.

7. Fiscal reform is underway, and the government has been piloting a municipal bond program since May 2014, which could have a significant impact in rationalizing China's fiscal system and addressing this issue. However, as of mid-February 2015, both fiscal reform and the municipal bond program remained in their early stages, while efforts to restrain local government borrowing (often conducted through opaque local government financing vehicles) were significantly more advanced.

8. This description somewhat elides the relationship between the CFELSG and the CDRLSG. The latter has six subgroups, one of which is focused on "economic system and ecological system" reforms. The office of this group is coheaded by Liu He and NDRC Director Xu Shaoshi, and is closely related but not perfectly overlapping with the CFELSG. For more details on this arrangement, see Naughton, "'Deepening Reform.'"

9. Gabriel Wildau, "China's anti-corruption probe broadens into finance sector," *Financial Times*, February 3, 2015, http://www.ft.com/intl/cms/s/0/e50b1036-ab73-11e4-8070-00144feab7de.html.

10. Lu Hui, "Xi explains China's reform plan," Xinhua, November 15, 2013, http://news.xinhuanet.com/english/china/2013-11/15/c_132891949.htm.

Moreover, it has done so without creating countervailing positive incentives for more active implementation.[11]

This effect is enhanced by another persistent characteristic of traditional policymaking: the vagueness of top-level documents. The Third Plenum resolution, for example, is a "vision statement with a to-do list," designed to establish the "general line" and overall "guiding ideology" for reform, but not to lay out its technical details.[12] These fall to the line agencies and local governments to promulgate and implement. In the right circumstances, this vagueness creates vital space for innovation in generating new local reform initiatives and making tweaks to top-level edicts to better suit them to local conditions. However, it can also provide an excuse for local officials to hide behind the contradictions inevitably embedded in the dialectical language of official party documents: announcing their support for the general line and giving the impression of sincere activity, while stalling on implementation of specific measures. Much of this is evident today.

At the same time, it is clear that Xi and current leadership are attempting to shift officials' incentive structures in favor of reform. For example, underneath the CDRLSG there are over 800 corresponding reform leading groups located within central government agencies and down to the prefectural level, each headed by the top-ranking party official in that body.[13] This unprecedented move was clearly designed to strengthen local accountability for reforms, as well as reporting arrangements between the center and localities. Reforms to the criteria used by the Central Committee Organization Department in conducting officials' annual evaluation have also been introduced. These reforms were designed to end "GDP obsession" and encourage more balanced local policy.[14] On the party side, Xi has pointedly sought to strengthen cadres' adherence to CCP rules, warning that they must "align themselves with the [Central Committee] in deed and thought, at all times, and in any situation."[15] Here the focus seems to be on reducing local leaders' incentives and ability to depart from central directives in policy implementation, and instead encouraging them to faithfully implement Beijing's vision for reform.

However, these structural reforms will take time to generate results, and their implementation represents a major technical as well as political challenge. Within China's unitary system, it is much easier to assess officials' performance using a clear, consistent, quantitative metric like GDP growth than their ability to "promote the formation of a unified market in which fair competition can take place."[16] Promoting a more hands-off approach to managing the economy more generally—while also strengthening the consistent application of standards, such as for food safety—will also require a culture shift and

11. Johnson, *Decoding China's Emerging "Great Power" Strategy in Asia*.
12. Naughton, "After the Third Plenum."
13. Naughton, "'Deepening Reform.'"
14. "China Focus: China's reformed official assessment hailed as landmark," Xinhua, December 11, 2013, http://news.xinhuanet.com/english/indepth/2013-12/11/c_132960340.htm.
15. "Xi stresses Party discipline, rules."
16. Li Keqiang, "On Deepening Economic Reform," *Qiushi* 6, no. 1 (October 2014), http://english.qstheory.cn/2014-11/02/c_1113067968.htm.

the cultivation of new capacities, regulations, and approaches. Such changes will inevitably take time.

All of this serves to underscore the challenges Xi faces, and to illustrate why much of the implementation of reform has been uncertain, uncoordinated, and unenthusiastic. However, it would be a mistake to take the progress made over two years as a final assessment of what is achievable over a decade. Xi and his allies have taken a running start at disrupting many of the formal and illicit incentive structures that underpinned China's old growth model. In doing so, they have shown they understand the centrality of incentives in shaping policy, recognized the old system was misaligned, and are demonstrating their determination to generate new incentives to encourage the comprehensive deepening of reform—even if they are not yet certain what these incentives will be. Moreover, these and other reforms, such as those in the legal system, illustrate that Xi's economic reform agenda is not just economic policy. As discussed below, the Third Plenum resolution is as much about comprehensive governance reforms, designed to strengthen the party's ability to effectively lead China further toward the great rejuvenation of the Chinese nation, and should be read in this context.

# Comprehensive, Inconclusive

Since assuming the leadership of the CCP, Xi has stressed as his overarching goal the realization of the "China Dream," defined as "the great rejuvenation of the Chinese nation."[17] In his explanation of the Third Plenum resolution a year later, he went on to explicitly link his updated vision of reform and opening with the overarching goal of achieving China's rejuvenation.[18] Giving the market a "decisive role" and establishing a "proper relationship between the market and government" are at the core of this agenda.

As the midpoint of Xi's first five-year term in office nears, a central question about the implementation of this reform agenda remains unanswered. On the one hand, the so-far incremental, experimental, and populism-tinged approach to economic reform may be evidence of opposition from vested interests, strong risk aversion, and general uncertainty. This would suggest reform is struggling amid "deeper waters." Alternatively, some evidence suggests Xi may be employing a sequenced strategy for achieving not only economic reform but also a complementary overhaul of China's current governance system. This would suggest that 2015 could well be a breakout year for reform. So far, the evidence as to which outcome is more likely remains inconclusive—though, to some degree, the answer will almost inevitably be "both."

On the former interpretation, it is clear that the Xi administration's approach to implementing substantive economic reform in its first two years has been incremental rather than decisive. With the exception of fiscal reform, where the CDRLSG has approved a

17. "Xi pledges 'great renewal of Chinese nation,'" Xinhua, November 29, 2012, http://news.xinhuanet.com/english/china/2012-11/29/c_132008231.htm.

18. Hui, "Xi explains China's reform plan."

comprehensive plan to be implemented by 2016, reforms even in identified priority areas have moved cautiously. In the case of finance, for example, draft rules for deposit insurance were introduced at the end of 2014, but a clear timeline for implementation, and for greater liberalization of deposit rates, remains unclear. The introduction of the Hong Kong–Shanghai Stock Connect was an important step toward openness, but China's capital account remains largely closed. In the area of SOE reform, the Third Plenum called for local governments to develop plans for converting public enterprises to "mixed ownership," and they have complied, but actual conversion pilots have moved slowly.[19] The CDRLSG has also approved reductions in the compensation packages for central SOE managers. This move could be an important sign that SOEs will be more closely managed moving forward, though it could also plausibly read as a populist measure to reduce perceptions of privilege rather than a substantive reform.[20]

Reliance on experimentation has also persisted from earlier eras, but with arguably more caution and less success than in the past. The Shanghai FTZ is the most high-profile example of this. Just 18 months into the experiment, the leadership has already begun to explore alternative strategies for building successful FTZs, having given permission in December 2014 for three additional provinces to establish their own zones. Capital account reforms have been largely absent in Shanghai, with those introduced featuring heavy emphasis on risk management over bold reforms. Even those initiatives most often cited as evidence of the Shanghai zone's success, notably the elimination of registered capital requirements for new firms (now policy nationwide), were not pilots unique to Shanghai, but measures simultaneously trialed elsewhere. While it remains premature to dismiss the Shanghai FTZ as a failure (and it is worth noting that the "negative list" approach to FDI represents a more significant shift in governance than is commonly recognized), the difficulties encountered in developing the zone present a microcosm of the overall challenge facing Chinese reform.

On the other hand, the same evidence cited above regarding the Xi administration's so-far uncertain, incremental, and experimental implementation style could be read differently: as the initial steps in a sequenced, strategic approach to comprehensive reform of not only China's economy, but its system of governance.[21] In other words, Xi could be preparing the ground for a "big swing" at decisive reforms.

---

19. There are some signs that SOE reform is gathering momentum. Reports in early 2015 from Xinhua and *Economic Information Daily* have indicated that an SOE reform package had been approved and was scheduled for release at the "two meetings" in March 2015. See "News Analysis: Policy design to propel China's SOE reforms," Xinhua, January 9, 2015, http://news.xinhuanet.com/english/china/2015-01/09/c_133909001.htm; Paul Pennay, "China gives green light for SOE reform package: Report," *China Spectator*, February 13, 2015, https://www.businessspectator.com.au/news/2015/2/13/china/china-gives-green-light-soe-reform-package-report; and "国企改革顶层方案或两会后出台," *Economic Information Daily*, February 13, 2015, http://jjckb.xinhuanet.com/2015-02/13/content_538313.htm.

20. Barry Naughton, "Leadership Transition and the 'Top-Level Design' of Economic Reform," *China Leadership Monitor*, no. 37 (Spring 2012), http://www.hoover.org/sites/default/files/uploads/documents/CLM37BN.pdf.

21. Arthur R. Kroeber, "Xi Jinping's Reform Express Gathers Steam," Brookings Institution, December 15, 2014, http://www.brookings.edu/research/opinions/2014/12/15-xi-jinpin-reform-kroeber.

Since the release of the Third Plenum resolution, many analysts have remarked on the impressive breadth of the reforms contained therein, while lamenting its failure to include precise time lines or a clear sense of priorities. This very breadth, they (correctly) point out, coupled with the endless idiosyncrasies of the Chinese economic system, make it difficult to benchmark or effectively assess the progress of reform. Nonetheless, for China to achieve major economic reform, while limiting the risk of major economic instability, such a comprehensive approach is undoubtedly necessary. Moving toward financial liberalization without first limiting implicit guarantees for state-linked borrowers would be courting disaster. Similarly, efforts to privatize much of China's enormous stock of public assets without first cracking down on corruption and strengthening supervision of local governments would be a recipe for a Russian-style selloff. Reforms in other areas are similarly intertwined.

Viewed in this light, the approach taken so far can be seen to make sense. Upon entering office, Xi focused immediately on dual anticorruption and mass-line campaigns, designed to clean up the party in practice and, to the extent possible, in the minds of the public. The campaigns also allowed Xi to solidify his position at the top of the party pile, and to assert greater control over the party's rank and file. He has since overseen the approval of China's first comprehensive fiscal reform plan since 1994, designed to clarify fiscal rights and responsibilities at all levels of government. If implemented, this will help tame China's local debt troubles, and reduce localities' reliance on land sales for revenue—a major source of risk and social unrest. Coupled with initially little-noticed legal reform initiatives introduced at the Fourth Plenum, aimed at taming the arbitrary exercise of power by local officials, and efforts to strengthen party discipline at all levels, these measures could together "make Chinese governance fairer, more transparent, and more responsive to citizens' concerns."[22] They would also help clear the way for more decisive reforms of China's financial system and SOEs, and create a more favorable environment for the growth and flourishing of a modern services sector.

While this strategic scenario and the alternative hesitant, incremental, and experimental interpretation articulated above each contain elements of truth, it is likely that neither is entirely accurate. Whichever way the balance tips, all available evidence suggests Xi Jinping is a leader of extraordinary ambition, deeply committed to achieving the "great rejuvenation of the Chinese nation" through the leadership of the Chinese Communist Party. This will make 2015 a critical year to watch for several reasons. Xi is two years into what is a presumed 10-year term. He has consolidated control over the key levers of power more decisively than any leader in decades. This leaves him with a window of opportunity to drive reform between now and when political jockeying in advance of the next party congress in 2017 begins in earnest. Given that the risks of delaying reform, whether from a slowing economy or rising debt, are continuing to mount with time, the present is as good a time as any—and better than most—for a major reform push.

---

22. Ibid.

# 7 Implications for Chinese Economic Reform

## China's Economic Challenges and the Imperative of Reform

China has reached the end of its days of double-digit growth.[1] The IMF projects the country's real GDP will grow below 7 percent in 2015, and even slower the year after.[2] This is an undisputed secular downturn. The size of China's labor force is shrinking and the country is aging.[3] The major gains from reallocating labor from agricultural to industrial activities have already been realized. China's overall debt-to-GDP ratio has risen to over 250 percent at a dizzying pace, and will likely continue to rise over the near term.[4] Further accumulation of capital, while necessary and desirable, will inevitably yield diminishing marginal returns to growth. By moving ever closer to the technological frontier, China has achieved dramatic productivity gains, but future gains will be harder to achieve.[5] Today, many aspects of the "hard" work of China's industrialization are complete: China has the world's largest high-speed rail network; the world's largest steel and cement industry; and three of the world's ten largest subway lines by length. The "soft" work of transforming China into a high-income economy—with modern services industries, modern regulatory systems, modern public services, and efficient, market-based resource allocation—is ongoing. The path ahead will be more treacherous.

These are only China's economic challenges. Beijing is also struggling to manage a host of social, environmental, and governance issues. On governance, as Xi himself has explained it, "China has to . . . work on the problems of an underdeveloped market system,

1. World Bank and Development Research Center of the State Council, People's Republic of China, *China 2030: Building a Modern, Harmonious, and Creative Society* (Washington, DC: World Bank, 2013), http://www.worldbank.org/content/dam/Worldbank/document/China-2030-complete.pdf.

2. International Monetary Fund (IMF), "World Economic Outlook: Update: Cross Currents," January 2015, https://www.imf.org/external/pubs/ft/weo/2015/update/01/index.htm.

3. Xin Zhou, "China's One-Child Policy Backfires as Labor Pool Shrinks Again," Bloomberg, January 20, 2015, http://www.bloomberg.com/news/articles/2015-01-20/china-s-one-child-policy-backfire-deepens-as-labor-pool-shrinks.

4. David Keohane, "ICYMI, China's credit buildup was pretty damn fast," *Financial Times*, January 26, 2016, http://ftalphaville.ft.com/2015/01/26/2100092/icymi-chinas-credit-buildup-was-pretty-damn-fast/; Wei Yao, "The Risks to China from Rapid Credit Growth," *Barron's*, January 30, 2015, http://online.barrons.com/articles/the-risks-to-china-from-rapid-credit-growth-1422612058.

5. World Bank and Development Research Center of the State Council, People's Republic of China, *China 2030*.

excessive government intervention, and weak supervision of the market."[6] Despite the country's rapid growth and rising living standards, dissatisfaction is widespread. Land seizures and illegal evictions by local governments remain common. Severe air pollution in major urban areas kills more Chinese every year than smoking,[7] rivers are polluted with runoff from coal mines and paper plants,[8] and safety scandals over food and consumer goods remain a regular occurrence.[9] Income inequality has risen sharply nationwide and deepened the divide between inland and coastal provinces, between rural and urban areas, and between the working migrant poor and entrenched local elites.

To address these challenges, the Xi Jinping administration has put forward China's most comprehensive reform agenda in decades. The 2013 Third Plenum resolution represents a bold vision statement for comprehensive reform, with a self-described goal of achieving major progress by 2020, and offers a to-do list for reaching these goals.[10] It promises to give markets a "decisive role" in resource allocation, "perfect a mixed public-private economy," and "build an ecological civilization."[11] Xi has simultaneously promised to fight corruption, restrict "power within the cage of regulations,"[12] and make innovation the driver of China's development.[13] Through so doing, Xi and his allies seek to transform China into a "moderately prosperous society" by 2020 and achieve the "China Dream" of the "great rejuvenation of the Chinese Nation" under the leadership of the Chinese Communist Party.[14]

Success will require implementing deep reforms in a country that has arguably endured more rapid, wrenching, and transformational change than any other over the past four decades. At its core, the Third Plenum reforms are about renegotiating the balance between the market and the state in economic affairs. Markets will need to be allowed a decisive role in allocating resources where they can do so most efficiently: for capital, for energy, and for labor. The state, even as it releases control in some areas, will gain new responsibilities and new powers, and face new expectations. Chinese citizens will continue

---

6. Lu Hui, "Xi explains China's reform plan," Xinhua, November 15, 2013, http://news.xinhuanet.com/english/china/2013-11/15/c_132891949.htm.

7. Li Jing, "Air pollution is bigger killer in China than smoking, says new Greenpeace study," *South China Morning Post*, February 4, 2015, http://www.scmp.com/news/china/article/1701625/air-pollution-bigger-killer-mainland-china-smoking-says-new-greenpeace.

8. Elizabeth C. Economy, *The River Runs Black: The Environmental Challenge to China's Future* (Ithaca, NY: Cornell University Press, 2010).

9. For example, Patrick Boehler, "Starbucks, Dicos withdraw sandwiches as China launches nationwide probe into 'rotten meat' firm," *South China Morning Post*, July 21, 2014, http://www.scmp.com/news/china/article/1556953/mcdonalds-kfc-supplier-closed-shanghai-authorities-investigate-rotten.

10. Naughton, "After the Third Plenum."

11. "The Decision on Major Issues Concerning Comprehensively Deepening Reforms in Brief," China.org.cn, November 16, 2013, http://www.china.org.cn/china/third_plenary_session/2013-11/16/content_30620736.htm.

12. "Xi Jinping vows 'power within cage of regulations,'" Xinhua, January 22, 2013, http://news.xinhuanet.com/english/china/2013-01/22/c_132120363.htm.

13. "Xi urges independent innovation in science, technology," Xinhua, June 9, 2014, http://news.xinhuanet.com/english/china/2014-06/09/c_133394743.htm.

14. "Xi pledges 'great renewal of Chinese nation,'" Xinhua, November 29, 2012, http://news.xinhuanet.com/english/china/2012-11/29/c_132008231.htm.

to ask for more from their government, and seek to hold it ever more accountable for deploying its power in a just and evenhanded manner.[15]

These changes will have enormous consequences for both 1.36 billion Chinese and the rest of the world. They give rise to the several questions that inspired this report:

- In a more pluralized political economy, are China's decisionmakers, its policymaking processes, and its institutions still well suited to transition China toward a "new normal" of strong, sustainable, and balanced growth?

- Can Zhongnanhai implement these reforms without triggering the wracking political and economic instability so many other developing and transitional economies have endured in the past?

- To what extent will the Communist Party be willing to give the market a truly "decisive role" in resource allocation—and, if it does so, what will the impact be on its continued power and legitimacy?

This last question reflects the underlying tension that animates China's reform agenda. The Xi administration has proposed giving the market a "decisive role" and relying more on innovation to drive China's growth. At the same time, it has overseen the most severe crackdown on the free flow of ideas and information in over two decades,[16] and worked to strengthen ideological indoctrination.[17] It has placed new restrictions on the use of foreign technology products and pressured foreign suppliers of high-tech goods to surrender access to their intellectual property in order to retain or gain entry to the Chinese market.[18] It would seem, in other words, that Beijing is putting to the test whether there is a contradiction between authoritarian party politics and the "modern, harmonious, and creative high-income society" that China hopes to become.

# Implications of the Xi Administration's Policymaking Style

As stressed throughout this report, the Xi administration's style of policymaking demonstrates both continuity and change with respect to earlier eras. Indeed, while Xi's approach is a departure from that of the Hu-Wen era, Xi in many ways appears to be drawing from the playbook of former premier Zhu Rongji in how he has gone about pursuing reform.

---

15. David M. Lampton, "How China Is Ruled," *Foreign Affairs* 93, no. 1 (January/February 2014), http://www.foreignaffairs.com/articles/140344/david-m-lampton/how-china-is-ruled.

16. Helen Gao, "China Sharpens Its Censorship Blade," *New York Times*, February 2, 2015, http://www.nytimes.com/2015/02/03/opinion/china-sharpens-its-censorship-blade.html.

17. Catherine Wong Tsoi-lai, "Marxism key to problem solving: Xi," *Global Times*, January 26, 2015, http://www.globaltimes.cn/content/903934.shtml.

18. Simon Denyer, "Why Internet users all around the world should be worried about China's Great Firewall," *Washington Post*, February 2, 2015, http://www.washingtonpost.com/blogs/worldviews/wp/2015/02/02/why-internet-users-all-around-the-world-should-be-worried-about-chinas-great-firewall/.

Zhu was the architect of China's last major reform push in the late 1990s and early 2000s, widely viewed as successful.[19] Why did his approach succeed? One factor was Zhu himself: experienced as both a politician and a technocrat; hard-driving, sharp, smart, and decisive; an evidence-based decisionmaker endowed with his own firm and comprehensive vision for reforming the Chinese economy. Another was Zhu's close working relationship with the then general secretary Jiang Zemin in the critical several years following the 15th Party Congress in 1997.[20] Jiang gave Zhu the political cover needed to decisively pursue wrenching reforms—and, when necessary, reined him in.[21] A third factor was the institutions that Zhu adapted or established, such as the Central Financial Work Commission, the State Commission for Restructuring the Economy, and the State Council WTO Work Leading Group.[22] He directly supervised these bodies and empowered talented teams of technocrats to aggressively drive forward reform. Finally, Zhu was helped by events abroad and external pressure. Specifically, the 1997 Asian financial crisis strengthened the conviction among Chinese policymakers that reform was urgently required. This helped to empower Zhu, who seized on the process of China's WTO accession as a vital source of external pressure with which to bludgeon vested interests into line.

The Xi administration's approach to economic reform illustrates some of these same characteristics: rapid, personalized, top-level decisionmaking; a comprehensive reform agenda with strong political backing; tailoring of policymaking institutions to support said agenda; and strong external pressure.

- By introducing a comprehensive market-oriented reform blueprint at the Third Plenum, top leaders in Beijing demonstrated that they understood China's economic challenges. They identified the fundamental problem—that the government interferes too much in resource allocation—and through the resolution's comprehensive sweep illustrated a keen grasp of the essential interrelatedness between key reform areas, from anticorruption to China's fiscal and financial systems.

- Xi has invested the Third Plenum agenda with his personal prestige as well as that of the Central Committee. Through skillful wielding of party ideology, he has also given it ironclad official legitimacy. As CSIS scholar Christopher Johnson has phrased it, to openly oppose the resolution to give markets a "decisive role" would be "to suggest that the CCP's overall ideological line is somehow in error. There is arguably no more serious charge in the CCP's political culture."[23]

---

19. Barry Naughton, "Zhu Rongji: The Twilight of a Brilliant Career," *China Leadership Monitor*, no. 1 (Winter 2002), http://media.hoover.org/sites/default/files/documents/clm1_BN.pdf.

20. For a variety of reasons, this relationship did deteriorate somewhat in the later years of the 15th Central Committee, leading to a notably sharp divide at the time of the 16th Party Congress.

21. "Chinese Economic Reform: Past, Present and Future" (conference, Brookings Institution, Washington, DC, January 9, 2015), http://www.brookings.edu/events/2015/01/09-chinese-economic-reform-zhu-rongji.

22. Yong Wang, "China's Stakes in WTO Accession: The Internal Decision-making Process," in *China's WTO Accession: National and International Perspectives*, ed. Heike Holbig and Robert Ash (London: RoutledgeCurzon, 2002).

23. Johnson, *Decoding China's Emerging "Great Power" Strategy in Asia*.

- Through key party leading groups, Xi has demonstrated his ability to engineer structural solutions at the apex of decisionmaking to get around China's gridlocked state bureaucracy. While not a technocrat himself, he has elevated and empowered a trusted and talented team of economic policymakers to oversee the reform agenda. His chosen advisers, such as Liu He, are known as capable and eloquent advocates of market-oriented reform, and key technocrats—notably Lou Jiwei and Zhou Xiaochuan—were even Zhu's subordinates during the last reform push.[24] They are powerful intellects and skilled bureaucratic navigators in their own right.
- China faces strong external pressure to pursue market reforms. This stems in particular from U.S. efforts to complete a TPP, as well as ongoing negotiations on a U.S.-China BIT. While the reforms required to conclude the BIT are not as sweeping as those necessitated by China's WTO accession, many of the necessary changes in Chinese governance—such as the shift from an approval-based to an ex-post supervision-based regulatory model for FDI—represent reforms with potentially far-reaching implications.

These signs augur well for China's reform prospects, but they do not guarantee success. There are also important differences between Zhu and Xi's policymaking styles. In sharp contrast to Xi's party-centered approach, Zhu consistently emphasized the role of the state in economic policymaking, and spent significant time and energy working to strengthen and modernize its institutions. By moving in the opposite direction, Xi is addressing the problem of gridlock that had emerged under his predecessors, but there is also clear potential for unintended consequences to emerge from this approach.

The substantive difference between the challenges and political economy facing Xi relative to Zhu are also clear. The Chinese economy is more than four times as large as when Zhu began implementing his reform agenda, and far more complex. In the past, China could rely on investment and exports to grow out of its challenges, but no such option exists today. Instead, it must look to the service sector as the chief driver of growth.[25] While it has substantial room to grow, creating a permissive environment will be a major challenge. Perhaps most importantly, in Zhu's time, there remained a strong national consensus behind growth as an overarching ambition. In the pluralized political economy of the present, there is no comparable unifying objective.

# Obstacles to Successful Implementation

Noted China scholar Barry Naughton has observed that there are three major risks to reform moving forward: that the reforms will stall or stumble on opposition; that they will

24. Barry Naughton, "Since the National People's Congress: Personnel and Programs of Economic Reform Begin to Emerge," *China Leadership Monitor*, no. 41 (Spring 2013), http://www.hoover.org/sites/default/files/uploads/documents/CLM41BN.pdf.

25. Ryan Rutkowski, "Services Sector Reform in China," Peterson Institute for International Economics Policy Brief No. 15-2, January 2015, http://www.piie.com/publications/pb/pb15-2.pdf.

be overtaken by events; or that the reform strategy itself will fail.[26] This provides a useful lens for examining likely obstacles to successful implementation of reform.

- *On the prospect of reforms stalling*, much commentary on Chinese economic reform focuses on the challenges posed by vested interests, in public enterprises, in protected sectors, and within local governments and the bureaucracy.[27] These vested interests could put up fierce resistance to reform. Even as the Third Plenum resolution is strengthened by its breadth, without a clear organizing principle and lacking a clear sense of priorities, it will be vulnerable to pushback from vested interests wielding deep insider knowledge.

  Xi alone will not have the bandwidth or expertise to counter such resistance by himself. Nor will Premier Li, or even Liu He. While Xi's chosen implementers will be essential in their own right, they will also need to rely on the professional bureaucracy for assistance in developing specific reform measures—or, at the least, for their compliance in implementing them. Yet the manner in which the Third Plenum documents were drafted almost certainly frustrated some in the bureaucracy.[28] A lack of strong bureaucratic support or particularly fierce resistance from vested interests could result in the reform agenda being nicked to death by a thousand cuts.

- *On reforms being overtaken by events*, it is clear that the major risk to China's economic outlook stems from rising leverage in the overall economy and the potential for some form of financial crisis. Most analysts believe this is not an imminent risk, and measures introduced over the past 18 months have succeeded in slowing China's rate of overall credit growth; however, credit continued to expand at a rate around double that of GDP in 2014.[29] In this context, an overly incremental, risk-averse approach to reform is a risk in and of itself, raising the likelihood of an eventual crisis.

  There is also political risk in delay. While in the broadest sense the need for and nature of reform may seem obvious, the agenda is contentious in its details. Should experiments like the Shanghai FTZ or other incremental measures fail to show results—or, even worse, generate instability—they could spawn a backlash against reform. Arguably the establishment of more than 800 local clones of the Communist Party's new Comprehensively Deepening Reform Leading Small Group, each competing to show its commitment to the new "vision statement," has further elevated the risk that ill-conceived measures may be introduced.[30]

---

26. Naughton, "After the Third Plenum."

27. Brian Spegele, "Are Chinese Leaders Ready to Take on Vested Interests?," *Wall Street Journal*, November 11, 2013, http://blogs.wsj.com/chinarealtime/2013/11/11/are-chinese-leaders-ready-to-take-on-vested-interests/; and Keyu Jin, "Reforms will stall unless Beijing tackles vested interests," *South China Morning Post*, January 27, 2015, http://www.scmp.com/comment/insight-opinion/article/1693301/reforms-will-stall-unless-beijing-tackles-vested-interests.

28. Johnson, *Decoding China's Emerging "Great Power" Strategy in Asia*.

29. Mark Mangier, "China Bank Move Leaves Companies Cold," *Wall Street Journal*, February 5, 2015, http://www.wsj.com/articles/china-bank-move-leaves-companies-cold-1423137091.

30. Naughton, "Since the National People's Congress."

- *On the prospect of the reform strategy failing*, China's top-down Leninist political system often sits uncomfortably astride China's mostly modern, mostly market economy. The system is designed to inhibit rather than enable effective horizontal and cross-regional coordination, and its tiered, top-down evaluation structure relies on centrally established metrics to assess official performance. Along with social stability, GDP growth has historically been chief among these metrics. As discussed earlier, GDP targets had unique value in terms of aligning central and local incentives and will be difficult to replace. Moreover, in the present pluralized political economy, it is possible that Chinese officials do not have the capacity or tools available to flexibly address Chinese society's growing variety of demands.

Lastly, as Naughton points out,[31] the central vision of the Third Plenum resolution is rebalancing the role of the market and the state to reduce distortions in the allocation of resources. However, Xi Jinping is also seeking to strengthen the central government's ability to enforce a top-level design of reform. There is a tension between these two trends, one toward more democratized economic decisionmaking, and one in the direction of greater central control. An additional challenge will lie in ensuring that whatever reforms are introduced, they are supported by institutional reforms to ensure that they are sustained. For example, to support fair competition and consistent regulation will require not only a temporary crackdown on local approvals, but sustained supervision to see they do not reemerge.

## Progress Likely, but Risks Abound

While the hurdles to successful reform are high, it would be a mistake to count China's leaders out. When it comes to generating and sustaining economic growth, successive generations of Chinese decisionmakers have proven themselves adaptable and pragmatic adherents to two of Deng Xiaoping's most famous sayings: "It doesn't matter whether a cat is black or white, as long as it catches mice," and "Seek truth from facts." Xi and his administration have demonstrated a level of ambition and urgency in pursuing reform not seen in over a decade. They have gathered a core cadre of respected economic policymakers to help guide them, sought advice from a global community of experts to inform their decisionmaking, and made dedicated efforts to learn from their own history and the experiences of other countries.

They also have advantages in pushing reform enjoyed by few other regimes. Xi and his colleagues in Zhongnanhai may face a more pluralized policymaking environment, but they also maintain control over all major levers of power in the Chinese political system. They have access to enormous financial resources and considerable space for near-term fiscal and monetary easing.[32] They have powerful tools available to sideline potential

31. Naughton, "After the Third Plenum."

32. IMF, "People's Republic of China: 2012 Article IV Consultation," IMF Country Report No. 12/195, July 2012, https://www.imf.org/external/pubs/ft/scr/2012/cr12195.pdf.

opponents of reform, ranging from anticorruption investigations and personnel appointments to information control and an enormous internal security apparatus.

Overall, Beijing's policymakers have a better-than-even chance of navigating the Chinese economy toward a new model of sustainable, consumption-led growth and achieving their own goal of "major progress" on the Third Plenum reform agenda by 2020. Even in this scenario, growth will continue to slow—an optimistic estimate in 2020 would be for 6 percent potential growth[33]—but this slower growth will likely be more balanced and therefore more sustainable.

However, an underlying risk to this outlook is how Xi's agenda beyond the economic realm will impact China's economic performance. Specifically, even as Beijing is pursuing "reform and opening," the party's search for "comprehensive security" is generating a countervailing impulse toward retrenchment and restriction. This is evident in aggressive ongoing campaigns to crack down on the free flow of information and ideas, strengthen ideological indoctrination (and purge "Western values"),[34] and "indigenize" China's information technology infrastructure. All of these efforts are likely to make China a more closed society and relations with trading partners more contentious, even as Beijing is seeking greater economic integration with the world economy. Moreover, beyond their social and political ramifications, these trends could have enormous negative consequences for China's future productivity growth, its ability to innovate and produce unique Chinese intellectual property, the quality of its overall business environment, and its ability to attract and retain top talent. The central tension between Xi's grasp for greater political control, on one hand, and the imperative of "letting go" economically, on the other, will continue to put a cloud over China's growth trajectory in the coming years.

33. Daniel H. Rosen, *Avoiding the Blind Alley* (Washington, DC: Asia Society Policy Institute, 2014), http://asiasociety.org/policy-institute/china-economy.

34. Chris Buckley, "China Warns Against 'Western Values' in Imported Textbooks," *New York Times*, January 30, 2015, http://sinosphere.blogs.nytimes.com/2015/01/30/china-warns-against-western-values-in-imported-textbooks/; Donald Clarke, "Shen Kui and his Three Questions," *Chinese Law Prof Blog*, January 31, 2015, http://lawprofessors.typepad.com/china_law_prof_blog/2015/01/shen-kui-and-his-three-questions.html.

# 8 Recommendations for the U.S. Government

The central question underlying this study—do China's policymakers today have the "right stuff" to successfully navigate a challenging transition to a new model of sustainable economic growth?—is more than an academic one for the United States. In fact, the answer will have far-reaching consequences for U.S. prosperity and security over the coming decades. Whether Beijing succeeds or fails in its efforts, the trajectory of the world's second-largest economy will have a substantial impact on the prospects for U.S. growth, as well as for American policy interests in and beyond the economic realm.

Thus policymakers in Washington have a significant stake in understanding economic decisionmaking dynamics in China, both their enduring characteristics and their evolution under the administration of Xi Jinping. This will enhance U.S. officials' ability to assess the prospects for Chinese economic reform and sustained growth. It will also better enable Washington to pursue policies that maximize U.S. interests in its relations with China, particularly as Beijing increasingly asserts itself as a regional and global power.

More broadly, Washington needs a new mindset in dealing with the China of 2015 and beyond. This is not the China of a decade ago, nor is it just another country with which the United States has a few commercial opportunities to be seized and tensions to be managed. China poses unique risks, challenges, and opportunities for the United States. After 35 years of rapid growth, China has resumed its historical place as the largest economy in Asia and will soon be the largest in the world by any measure; no other economy will have more impact on U.S. growth and prosperity over the coming decades. At the same time, Beijing has made clear that it intends to play a greater role in the regional and global order. Vice Premier Wang Yang has insisted, "A growing China poses no threat to America's leading role in today's world."[1] Yet China's rise will inevitably disrupt American leadership of the global order that has prevailed over the past 70 years.

Thus senior U.S. policymakers need to devote more time, resources, and policy bandwidth to China than they have to date. What is needed today is akin to the broad mobilization of the U.S. government during the Cold War—though of course China is not the Soviet Union, and the objective is not containment but rather informed, proactive engagement. It

1. "Chinese vice premier urges U.S. to treat China with 'strategic foresight,'" Xinhua, December 18, 2014, http://news.xinhuanet.com/english/china/2014-12/18/c_133863755.htm.

will not be enough to add a Mandarin speaker or two in each government agency, or to gear up the policy machinery once a year ahead of a presidential visit. Instead, the U.S. policymaking apparatus needs to be systematically enhanced to deal with the ongoing challenges and opportunities of a country that will be America's principal global competitor—and a potential partner—in the decades ahead.

Substantively, Washington's economic policies toward China should be aimed at two broad objectives: first, incentivizing Beijing to play by established rules, both in maintaining an open, level playing field at home and in supporting the global rules–based economic order; and second, encouraging Beijing to continue reform and rebalancing of its economy toward sustainable, consumption-led growth. A stable, growing, rule-abiding China is in America's best interest.

An effective economic strategy toward China begins with leading from strength. This means Washington must pursue sound macroeconomic and structural policies that support strong, sustainable, balanced U.S. growth. It means having strategic foreign economic policies that build on our national advantages and enlist our allies in support of shared interests and values. It means deploying the resources to back up these strategies. It means following through on our commitments—notably governance reform of the Bretton Woods institutions—to give the United States the credibility it requires to remain a leader in global economic affairs.

We offer below a number of specific recommendations to the U.S. government about managing economic policy toward China. In keeping with the procedural and institutional focus of this study, these are organizational suggestions divided into two broad categories: engaging with China, and organizing the U.S. government.

# Engaging with China

1. *Support China's economic reforms where they align with U.S. interests.* Of course, China will be guided in its economic decisionmaking first and foremost by its own interests, not by U.S. preferences. The good news is that many of the reforms Beijing is pursuing would advance the U.S. objectives of more balanced growth in China and a more level playing field. From an American perspective, there is much that is consistent with U.S. priorities in the "Decision" document released at the Third Plenum in 2013: giving the market a decisive role in the Chinese economy; prioritizing financial reform, which is key to better resource allocation and more consumption-led growth; and subjecting SOEs to greater market discipline.

   In their public statements and in interactions with Chinese counterparts, U.S. officials should offer support whenever appropriate to the positive elements of China's reform program. This can build goodwill (up to a point). It can also bolster advocates of reform within the Chinese system. As this study has shown, despite the impression of Chinese policymaking as monolithic, the reality is that numerous actors are vying for policy influence in an increasingly pluralized political economy. Some of these actors have interests that are aligned with those of the United States—albeit for their own reasons. U.S. policymakers should identify and focus on the benefits to these actors in their messaging, while being careful not to taint them by explicit association with American interests.

A related point is that, when making requests for policy changes that advance U.S. interests, Washington should link these to Beijing's own declared reform plans. A "win-win" argument is more likely to sway a Chinese official than one put forward from a parochial U.S. perspective. For example, Washington has long made the case that Beijing would benefit from boosting household income and transitioning toward a more consumption-led growth model. This argument has gained significant traction with time, and engineering this transition has been made a central objective of the Xi administration's overall reform agenda.

2. *Challenge Beijing when its policies are out of step with U.S. interests—pressure can work.* There is a popular view among U.S. commentators that Beijing keeps its own counsel, has little concern for what outsiders—especially the U.S. government—say, and does not respond well to outside criticism. Like most conventional wisdom, there is some validity to this view, but the truth is more complicated. The fact is that pressure—defined broadly as both carrots and sticks—works in China, and the U.S. government should exploit it to advance its economic interests.

As this study has shown, one of the enduring characteristics of Chinese economic decisionmaking is Beijing's use of external competitive pressure to drive domestic economic reform. Soon after Japan joined the TPP negotiations in 2013, the Xi Jinping administration appears to have seized on this tool, much as Zhu Rongji did with WTO accession in the 1990s, to soften resistance to pending Third Plenum reforms. The BIT negotiations with the United States may be playing a similar role at the moment, with the added "carrot" that Beijing is seeking more certainty for its investors in the United States. From a U.S. perspective, this makes initiatives like TPP and the BIT powerful tools not only to promote market-based reform in China but also to incentivize China to deepen its integration in the global rules–based order. (This point is discussed further in recommendations 7 and 8 below.) By better understanding internal decisionmaking processes and policy objectives in China—in other words, knowing what Beijing wants and how it reacts to external pressure—Washington can use these incentives to shape Beijing's policy behavior.

The stick can also be effective. The United States has a number of commercial grievances with China, from long-standing concerns like intellectual property rights violations and currency manipulation to newer complaints about cyber theft and regulatory harassment of U.S. investors via implementation of the anti-monopoly law. These problems are far from being solved, but Washington has made progress in chipping away at them through a range of bilateral and global tools, from prioritizing them in the Joint Commission on Commerce and Trade (JCCT) to pursuing WTO dispute-settlement cases. This kind of pressure should be applied whenever it would clearly advance U.S. interests. Moreover, by working with allies to shape rules and norms for economic activity—including by filing joint WTO cases—Washington can shift Beijing's calculus in favor of compliance even when the two capitals disagree.

In using pressure and incentives, Washington should ensure consistency of messaging, both over time and among different elements of the U.S. government; Chinese officials are quick to pick up on and exploit inconsistencies in U.S. positions. The National Security Council (NSC) should ensure that all senior agency officials work from a common set of messages. A related issue is that Washington should be smarter about publicly responding to Chinese actions that cause it concern; the moody silence following Beijing's announcement of an Asian infrastructure bank in the summer of 2014 allowed others to portray Washington as blocking a reasonable-seeming Chinese initiative and twisting the arms of its allies behind the scenes.

3. *Ensure that Beijing engages at an appropriate political level.* As highlighted in this study, the U.S. and Chinese governments are structured very differently. While China's State Council notionally corresponds to the U.S. president's cabinet, the two are not equivalent in terms of actual policymaking functions, in two important ways. First, the State Council includes not only heads of government departments but also a tier of vice premiers and state councilors who outrank mere ministers. Second, the CCP—specifically, the seven-member PBSC—sits atop the decisionmaking pyramid in a way that no political party or steering group in the United States does.

   Thus ministers are not the political equivalent of U.S. cabinet officers, but more like senior departmental administrators. Ministers have little or no authority to effect policy change across the government—or in many cases even in their own area of jurisdiction. This means that in order to engage on policy matters at a political level, U.S. cabinet officers need to interact with vice premiers or state councilors with relevant responsibility.

   This was the organizational logic behind the original U.S.-China Strategic Economic Dialogue led by former treasury secretary Henry Paulson and its Obama administration successor, the Strategic and Economic Dialogue (S&ED). These forums enabled U.S. cabinet officers to sit across the table from their real peers, vice premiers and state councilors, who had been empowered to work across policy bailiwicks. Recommendation 6 below discusses the S&ED further, but the broader point is that Washington should take pains to identify appropriate senior interlocutors in China and use White House intervention to ensure that Beijing delivers the appropriate counterpart to U.S. cabinet officers and their delegates. Proper identification means not only getting the level right but ensuring appropriate substantive responsibility; for example, the S&ED currently has a mismatch in that Treasury Secretary Jacob Lew's counterpart, Wang Yang, does not have responsibility for most of the financial issues on the U.S. agenda. In reality, there may not always be a single ideal counterpart: under the Xi administration, different elements of the economics portfolio—for example, trade and finance—are scattered across several vice premiers.

In addition to established governmental counterparts, Washington should play closer attention to China's "leading small groups," especially the CFELSG. As this study has shown, these groups have taken on a significant new role in policy formulation under Xi Jinping. As Communist Party bodies, leading small groups are not formally accessible to U.S. policymakers. However, most key members of the groups are dual-hatted in senior governmental roles—for example, Liu He, director of the secretariat of the CFELSG, is also vice chairman of the NDRC—and can be approached in the latter capacity, including through the long-standing State Department–NDRC dialogue. To better understand China's decisionmaking processes and priorities, and potentially to shape policy outcomes, it is important that Washington have better line of sight into the leading small groups.

4. *Establish an informal back channel between the White House and Zhongnanhai.* The U.S.-China relationship, particularly in its economic dimensions, has reached a scope and significance that require more than episodic involvement of the two countries' leaders, principally via annual summit meetings. While significantly more frequent interaction between the leaders themselves is unrealistic, there should be more opportunities—at least twice a year—for quiet, informal dialogue among top proxies in the White House and Zhongnanhai. The purpose of this back channel would be to enhance trust between the two sides, reduce the scope for misunderstanding or miscalculation, anticipate problems, and engage on both opportunities and challenges in the relationship.

   A series of such interactions was held in the first term of the Obama administration, when the national security adviser and director of the National Economic Council met in alternating capitals with key advisers to the top Chinese leadership in corresponding policy areas. This is one model; other structures and participants are conceivable. But the lack of a top-level back channel in the late Obama and early Xi administrations has been noted with concern by observers on both sides, and such a channel should be established as a matter of course. At the same time, Washington should be wary of Beijing's preference for negotiating with "old friends" and avoid overreliance on personal guarantees to produce tangible outcomes. A team approach internally, and close coordination with U.S. allies (such as Australia, Japan, and South Korea), is essential to maximize the chances of positive outcomes.

5. *Pay more attention to center-local relationships.* A key feature of Chinese economic decisionmaking highlighted in this study is the tension between central and local levels of government. Given the critical role that provincial and subprovincial leaders in the Communist Party, government, and SOEs play in policy formulation and implementation, the U.S. government should do more to engage with these local leaders. This would help build understanding of local perspectives, support for U.S. policy objectives, and relationships with key decisionmakers—including the top tier of party officials who often go on to leadership roles in Beijing. Local leaders are likely to be more solicitous of inward direct investment than is Beijing and to have a

growing stake in investment opportunities in the United States for their local SOEs, which should make them receptive to this engagement.

Foreign Service, Foreign Commercial Service, and other officers posted at the five U.S. consulates around China already do vital work at the local level, as does the ambassador himself through his periodic travels around the country; all of this should be encouraged and expanded. Cabinet secretaries and other top officials visiting from Washington should also make more regular trips to the provinces to meet with key local governors and party officials. When American governors, mayors, and congressional delegations visit Chinese provinces—as they increasingly do—they should be briefed by senior policymakers in Washington before they travel and debriefed when they return. This is vital to ensure that these delegations understand the objectives and key points of the administration's China strategy and to allow senior policymakers to better understand what U.S. delegations are seeking to accomplish through their visits. Such strengthened engagement would also boost the consistency of American messaging, improve internal coordination, and potentially provide useful information on local affairs in China.

6. *Maintain but streamline the S&ED.* As noted in recommendation 3 above, the U.S.-China S&ED and its predecessor, the Strategic Economic Dialogue, have been useful innovations in management of the bilateral relationship. By involving an empowered vice premier and state councilor, the S&ED has served the important organizational function of ensuring top-level political engagement in Beijing on U.S. policy priorities. Substantively, the forum has been valuable in setting an agenda for bilateral discussion on key political and economic issues, managing short-term challenges in the relationship, and promoting longer-term cooperation. If the S&ED did not exist, something like it would need to be created.

   However, numerous observers—including CSIS in a 2013 report[2]—have pointed out that the S&ED has become unwieldy, involving half a dozen cabinet agencies and hundreds of U.S. government officials. Moreover, the annual gatherings have inevitably been driven more by short-term "deliverables" than by longer-term strategic issues. Our 2013 report offered some suggestions for streamlining the S&ED. As a practical matter, it may be too late at this point in the Obama and Xi terms to do a substantial overhaul of the forum, but a new administration in Washington in 2017 and President Xi at the start of his second term could consider ways to restructure the forum to make it more focused, substantive, and strategic.

7. *Keep BIT negotiations high on the bilateral agenda.* Washington and Beijing have been negotiating a bilateral investment treaty for several years, but this has recently become a top priority on the bilateral agenda. At the S&ED meeting in July 2014, the

2. Matthew P. Goodman et al., *Crafting Asia Economic Strategy in 2013* (Washington, DC: CSIS, January 2013), http://csis.org/files/publication/130123_Goodman_CraftingAsiaEconStrat_Web.pdf; "U.S.-China Trade and Economic Relations," in U.S-China Economic and Security Review Commission, *2014 Annual Report to Congress*, November 2014, http://origin.www.uscc.gov/sites/default/files/Annual_Report/Chapters/Chapter%20 1%20U.S.-China%20Economic%20and%20Trade%20Relations.pdf.

two governments agreed to accelerate the negotiations, after Beijing had agreed the previous year to adopt a "negative list" approach to investment approvals and to offer preestablishment national treatment for U.S. investors. Given the two countries' sometimes conflicting interests and different historical approaches to investment policy, progress in the negotiations has been understandably slow, and early completion of the agreement will be challenging. Moreover, even a completed BIT agreement will face a difficult political path to approval by the U.S Congress, particularly in light of concerns from both organized labor and parts of the business community.

Nevertheless, Washington should keep the BIT high on the bilateral agenda, for several reasons. First, it could help to address some of the growing concerns among U.S. investors about an increasingly unfriendly investment climate in China, including persistent equity restrictions, perceived bias in enforcement of the antimonopoly law, and preferential treatment of domestic champions. Also, China has a growing stake in direct investment in the United States and sees the BIT as a way of ensuring greater certainty for Chinese companies hoping to invest in the United States. (In fact, a BIT will do little to address one of China's long-standing concerns, i.e., the workings of the Committee on Foreign Investment in the United States [CFIUS], which screens investments that pose national security concerns; but inclusion of investor-state dispute settlement [ISDS] in a U.S.-China BIT would give Chinese investors recourse on investment barriers not related to national security.) Finally, a BIT could be a way station on the path to Chinese participation in TPP or a successor regional trade agreement, since it includes many of the investment-related disciplines at the core of TPP.

Thus the BIT serves many of the carrot-and-stick functions described in recommendation 2 above. While it is not a panacea, and the political calendars in both the United States and China in 2016–2017 mean the chances of a BIT agreement being completed and approved soon are very uncertain, the administration should continue to prioritize the negotiations as an incentive for Beijing to adopt a more level playing field in China and support the global rules–based order.

8. *Pursue a robust regional and global economic strategy.* The previous seven points focus on direct management of bilateral relations with China. A successful U.S. economic strategy toward China also requires robust engagement by Washington in institution-building and norm-setting in the Asia-Pacific region and globally. The goal of these efforts is to incentivize Beijing to promote market-based reform and work constructively within the existing rules-based order, by demonstrating that the order largely works for China.

   Regionally, the U.S. government should continue its longtime championing of the Asia-Pacific Economic Cooperation (APEC) forum and its more recent pursuit of a TPP trade agreement. Although underappreciated in Washington, APEC is an important part of the regional architecture: it is a consensus-based organization that does valuable pick-and-shovel work to deepen regional economic integration by bringing together officials from across the region—including China and the United States—to work on common economic challenges, from streamlining customs procedures to empowering women. Meanwhile, TPP is a self-described "high-standard, 21st century" trade negotiation that brings together the United States, Japan, and 10 other APEC economies (not yet including China).

APEC and TPP have recently proven their value in drawing China more deeply into the regional rules-based system. As APEC host in 2014, Beijing ultimately brokered a set of outcomes on regional trade and investment liberalization that were largely consistent with U.S. interests. With TPP nearing completion in 2015, Beijing has shown greater interest in the agreement (and in a broader Free-Trade Area of the Asia-Pacific [FTAAP], which would need to be built on TPP rules), because it sees many aspects of TPP's high standards as consistent with its own efforts to drive economic reform at home. Washington should continue to invest heavily in APEC and TPP as important strategic tools of its economic strategy toward China.

Meanwhile, at the global level, Washington should continue to use multilateral organizations and forums such as the WTO, the United Nations Framework Convention on Climate Change (UNFCCC), and the Group of 20 (G20) to seek cooperation from China in supporting and updating the global rules–based economic order. While Beijing has sometimes resisted specific norm-setting efforts by these bodies, or violated existing rules, it appears to recognize the value of these institutions in promoting Chinese interests, from driving reform at home to curbing greenhouse gas emissions; and, when challenged, Beijing has generally complied with the letter of its obligations in these organizations.

Yet Beijing's recent efforts to create parallel institutions such as the New Development Bank ("BRICS Bank") and Asian Infrastructure Investment Bank (AIIB) demonstrate an ambition to play a greater leadership role in global economic governance—with Chinese characteristics. To ensure that these efforts support the existing rules-based order and do not undermine it, Washington needs to follow through on its commitment to reform the governance and operations of existing Bretton Woods institutions and give China a greater voice in running them. An urgent priority is for the U.S. administration and Congress to work together to ratify quota and governance reforms at the International Monetary Fund.

Finally, Washington should work with its allies in Asia and Europe to ensure a united front on market-based economic reform in China and Beijing's support for the rules-based order. China does not like to be seen as an outlier and is more likely to be responsive to consistent messages from a number of countries, rather than just from the United States.

# Organizing the U.S. Government

9. *Prepare a presidential strategy document on China, with economic policy at the core.* China poses unique challenges and opportunities for the United States in the twenty-first century. Washington needs to think about how it deals with China differently from the way it deals with other countries, and differently from the way it has in the past. It needs to organize a more robust, better-resourced set of structures, processes, and policies that address all facets of the China challenge.

    The first step is for the White House to convene an interagency process to develop a comprehensive strategy on China that is codified in a National Security Presidential Directive or equivalent document. (Ideally this would include both a classified internal version and an unclassified version for public release.) The mere process of pulling U.S. government agencies together to go through this exercise would be useful, since it would underscore the priority that the White House places on China policy, allow for airing of agency views and experiences dealing with China in a number of cross-cutting policy areas, and help ensure that all agencies are aligned on strategy and messaging. Setting down the strategy in a presidential directive would help ensure consistency of approach across agencies and over time. As far as the authors of this report are aware, no such comprehensive written strategy on China has ever been produced by a U.S. administration, but the scope, scale, and complexity of U.S.-China relations today demand it.

10. *Prioritize senior White House engagement on China, including economic policy.* During the Cold War, U.S. presidents and their national security advisers (NSAs) considered it a matter of course to devote a substantial part of their foreign policy time to European affairs, and to visit the region several times a year if necessary to attend NATO summits or meetings with allies. By contrast, the White House today has relatively few resources devoted to Asia, with only one senior director in the NSC, focused primarily on political and security issues; and it is a significant scheduling challenge to get the president to Asia even once a year.

    Given that Asia is the world's largest economic region, containing the second- and third-largest economies, China and Japan; that the region is home to a number of critical security issues from North Korea's nuclear program to maritime tensions; and that China's growing regional role poses substantial challenges and opportunities for the United States, more senior policy time and resources in the White House on Asia, and especially China, are urgently called for.

    This starts at the top. It may be unrealistic to sustain two presidential trips to Asia every year, but the White House should plan on regular spring and fall meetings with the Chinese leader. The APEC and East Asia Summit meetings provide a reliable opportunity for a bilateral meeting in the fall; a regular spring summit in alternating capitals should be added to the presidential calendar. The leaders' meetings should be informal, and economics should be high on the agenda—focusing not only on pressing commercial issues but also on longer-term strategic topics like regional trade and investment architecture and global economic governance. It is important to consistently seek ways to keep these meetings fresh and avoid their becoming routinized or staff driven.

In addition to accompanying the president to the region, the NSA should find at least one other opportunity to go to China each year for the kind of back-channel dialogue discussed in recommendation 4 above. The NSA's role is not to replace the secretary of state in operational management of U.S.-China relations, but regular interaction with Chinese counterparts is essential. When in Washington, the NSA should give more share of mind to Asia and China—including economic strategy—as a matter of course.

To drive China economic strategy, the deputy NSA for international economics should convene a regular (at least monthly) "deputies group" of relevant senior officials from the State, Treasury, and Commerce departments, the U.S. Trade Representative's office, and other economic agencies (see also recommendation 11 below). The purpose would be to refine strategy and messaging and to ensure that agencies implement the strategy effectively and consistently.

Finally, improvements in White House organizational structure are called for to enhance coverage of Asian economic issues, especially longer-term strategic questions involving China. Jurisdiction for these issues in the NSC is currently divided between the Asia regional office and the international economics directorate, and neither has sufficient resources to handle the array of issues that arise. One tangible improvement would be to create a dedicated China economics director in the NSC who co-reports to the senior director for international economics and the senior director for Asia. The role of this officer—like all NSC officials—should *not* be to operationally manage U.S.-China economic relations, but to coordinate policy formulation and implementation by line agencies such as State and Treasury.

This is an issue of not only resources but mindset: senior White House policy officials from the president to the NSA to senior directors should treat China—including in the economic sphere—as the top priority that it is.

11. *Enhance China economic expertise—and accountability—in cabinet agencies.* Given the stakes for the United States in China's economic performance and policies, no economic agency of the U.S. government can afford to be without a deep bench of analysts and policy staff dedicated to China and Asia more broadly. The numbers are growing but remain inadequate to the task. Even the State Department, where the bulk of China expertise is appropriately housed, has gaps: after an organizational change early in the Obama administration, there is currently no deputy assistant secretary (DAS) in the Bureau of East Asia and Pacific Affairs responsible for economic issues; arguably there should be one DAS solely dedicated to U.S.-China economic relations. Other economic agencies such as Treasury and Commerce should

make recruiting and training of Asia policy experts a priority, and should consider beefing up their offices in China through secondments of State officers.

Moreover, each economic agency needs at least one official at deputy- or under-secretary level who is held accountable for steering the agency's contributions to China economic policy. This official need not be a China expert but should have a substantial portion of his or her portfolio focused on China issues, have sufficient staff dedicated to these issues, and be clearly designated as the point of contact with the White House, other agencies, and the Chinese government. (See also recommendation 10.)

12. *Work closely with Congress and other stakeholders (including business) to shape China economic strategy.* Effectively partnering with Congress and other stakeholders in the U.S.-China relationship is critical to any U.S. administration's economic strategy toward China. Congress of course provides the necessary resources to the administration and enacts trade and other relevant legislation that underpins the strategy. Several of the recommendations above would require additional funding—for example, more China economic officers at executive agencies—or legislative approval—for example, Senate advice and consent on a BIT.

Moreover, Congress can reinforce administration messaging regarding both China's domestic economic policy and support for the rules-based order, through oversight hearings, resolutions, and delegations to the country (including, as indicated in recommendation 5 above, provincial-level visits). For all of these reasons, senior administration officials should consult frequently with key members and staffers from both houses, both parties, and all relevant committees—those with jurisdiction over foreign affairs as well as finance and commerce. This should include mutual briefings before and after trips to China, as well as around visits by senior Chinese officials to the United States.

A similarly comprehensive approach should be used in coordinating with other stakeholders, and the business community in particular. Successive U.S. administrations have consistently advocated on behalf of American commercial interests with the Chinese government. Ensuring that the administration has strong channels to receive input from businesses, and that business is aligned with U.S. policy priorities, is essential to a comprehensive and successful economic strategy toward China.

# Appendix I: The Comprehensively Deepening Reform Leading Small Group

The 23-member Comprehensively Deepening Reform Leading Small Group (CDRLSG) is a party body established following the Third Plenum of the 18th Central Committee. It is tasked with oversight of China's overall reform agenda and ensuring "major progress" on reform by 2020 (when its remit theoretically expires). Between its official establishment on December 30, 2013 and mid-February 2015, the CDRLSG held nine meetings. In a first for a body of this type, portions of these meetings have been shown on Chinese state television, providing unusual insight into its membership. According to public releases, measures approved by the CDRLSG range from a comprehensive fiscal reform plan to measures for encouraging the development of "think tanks with Chinese characteristics." Despite its high profile, as is the case for central LSGs more generally, the internal procedures of the CDRLSG are not publicly disclosed.

As illustrated below, the CDRLSG is headed by Xi Jinping, and three additional members of the PBSC serve as vice chairmen—including Liu Yunshan, China's propaganda czar. The CDRLSG's general office is housed within the Central Policy Research Office and headed by Politburo member Wang Huning. The body also has six subgroups, including one focused on "Economic Structure and Ecological Reform," which is jointly headed by NDRC Director Xu Shaoshi and NDRC Deputy Director Liu He. Out of the 336 initiatives contained within the Third Plenum document, 181 have been delegated to one of these six groups. Of those measures so far delegated, the economics group is responsible for 118. In an unprecedented institutional innovation, beneath the central CDRLSG, there are more than 800 corresponding groups located within functional agencies and down to the prefectural level of government. These are headed by the highest-ranking party official within each administrative unit.

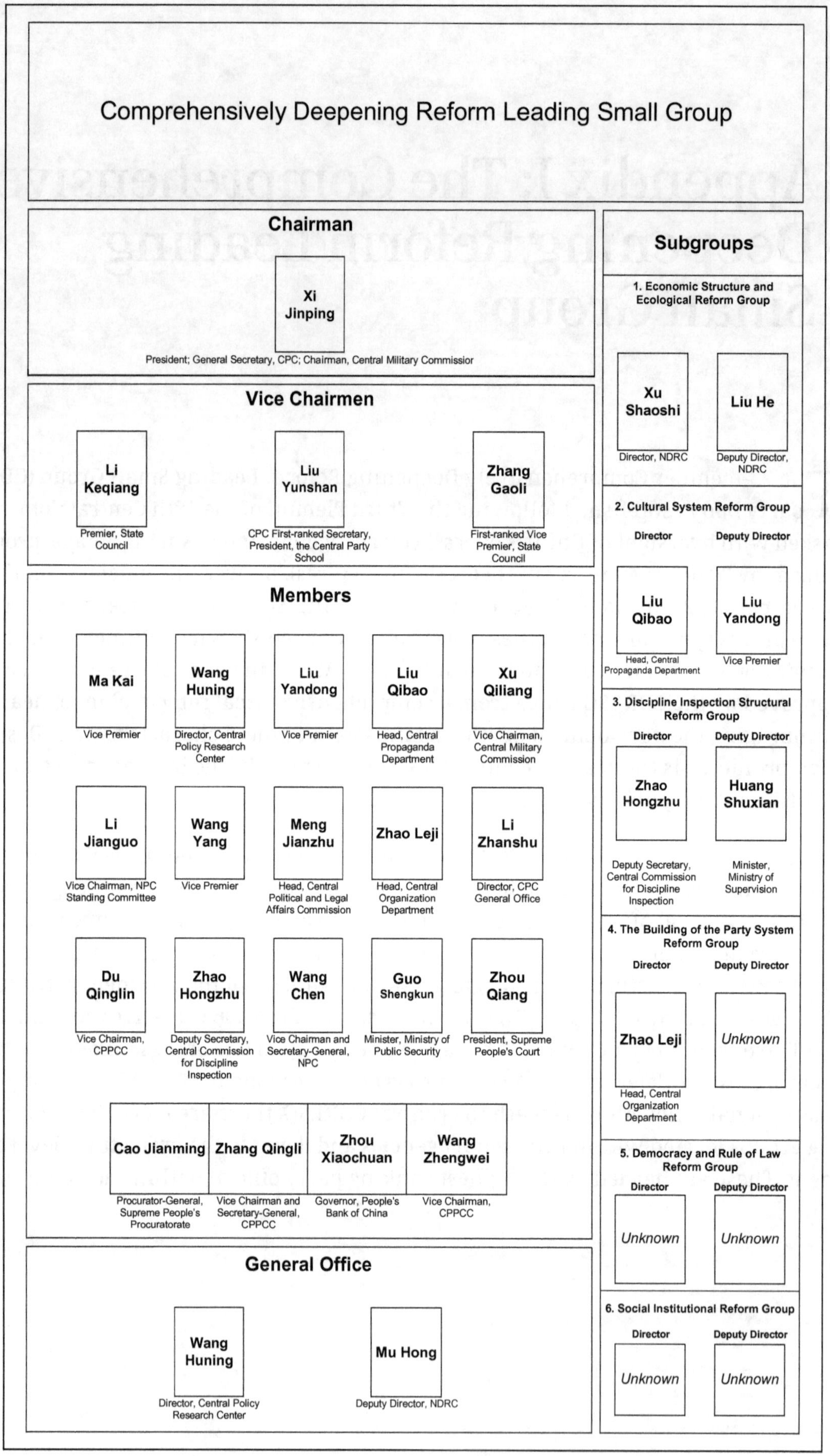


Note: As of February 2015.

# Appendix II: The Central Finance and Economics Leading Small Group

## Chairman

**Xi Jinping**
President; General Secretary, CPC; Chairman, Central Military Commission

## Vice Chairman

**Li Keqiang**
Premier, State Council

## Members

| | | | | | |
|---|---|---|---|---|---|
| **Liu Yunshan**<br>First-ranked Secretary, CPC Central Committee; President, the Central Party School | **Zhang Gaoli**<br>First-ranked Vice Premier, State Council | **Liu Yandong**<br>Vice Premier, State Council | **Wang Yang**<br>Vice Premier, State Council | **Ma Kai**<br>Vice Premier, State Council | **Wang Huning**<br>Director, Central Policy Research Center |
| **Li Zhanshu**<br>Director, CPC General Office | **Yang Jiechi**<br>State Councilor, State Council | **Yang Jing**<br>Secretary, CPC Central Committee; Secretary-General, State Council | **Zhou Xiaochuan**<br>Governor, People's Bank of China | **Fang Fenghui**<br>Chief of General Staff, PLA | **Xiao Jie**<br>Deputy Secretary-General, State Council |
| **Xu Shaoshi**<br>Director, NDRC | **Miao Wei**<br>Minister, Ministry of Industry and Information Technology | **Jiang Daming**<br>Minister, Ministry of Land and Resources | **Jiang Weixin**<br>Minister, Ministry of Housing and Urban-Rural Development | **Chen Lei**<br>Minister, Ministry of Water Resources | **Liu He**<br>Deputy Director, NDRC |
| **Wang Yi**<br>Minister, Ministry of Foreign Affairs | **Wang Zhigang**<br>Vice Minister, Ministry of Science and Technology | **Lou Jiwei**<br>Minister, Ministry of Finance | **Zhou Shengxian**<br>Minister, Ministry of Environmental Protection | **Yang Chuantang**<br>Minister, Ministry of Transport | **Wu Xinxiong**<br>Director, National Energy Administration<br>*Retired 12/2014* |

## General Office

| Director | Deputy Directors | | | | |
|---|---|---|---|---|---|
| **Liu He**<br>Deputy Director, NDRC | **Chen Xiwen**<br>Director, Agricultural Affairs Office under the State Council | **Yang Weimin**<br>Vice Minister, Ministry of Science and Technology | **Yi Gang**<br>Vice Governor, People's Bank of China; Director, SAFE | **Han Jun**<br>*Currently has no additional appointments* | **Shu Guozeng**<br>*Currently has no additional appointments* |

Note: As of February 2015.

The 26-member Central Finance and Economics Leading Small Group (CFELSG) is a party body first established in 1957. It has existed continuously since March 1980. The CFELSG's role in overall economic decisionmaking and composition have varied across generations of China's leadership. Under the Xi administration, it is playing an unusually large role in overseeing China's economic reform agenda. Much of the drafting of the reform plan released in November 2013 at the Third Plenum was performed by officials seconded from the CFELSG. The drafting committee was chaired by Xi Jinping and composed of other top leaders—including fellow PBSC members Liu Yunshan and Zhang Gaoli—as well as key experts. In a further illustration of its current importance, in the past the CFELSG has been chaired by the premier, but at present Xi himself heads the body and Li Keqiang serves as vice chair.

The CFELSG's general office director is Liu He, and five deputy directors have so far been revealed. Reports suggest that under Xi, the staff of this office has expanded considerably, in keeping with its new functional role as the secretariat for overseeing and implementing the overall reform agenda. As of mid-February 2015, official reports indicate the full CFELSG had held nine meetings since the beginning of the Xi administration, the last five of which have been publicly reported. The announcement of these meetings, as well as confirmation of the CFELSG's composition, is unprecedented for an LSG, the membership and meetings of which are typically not disclosed. Topics discussed at meetings so far include the Asian Infrastructure Investment Bank and the "One Belt, One Road" strategy, as well as China's innovation and energy security strategies.

# Appendix III: China's Formal Government Structure

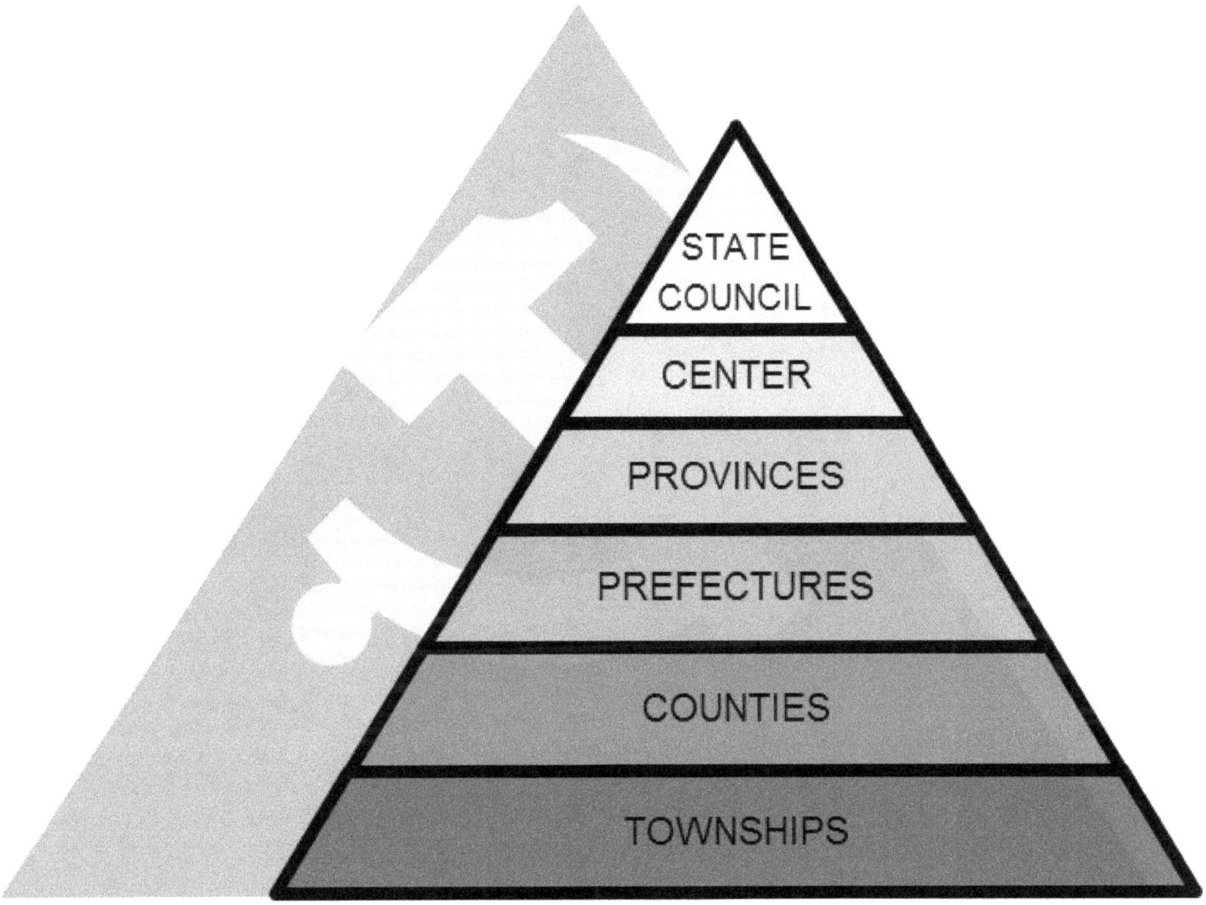


This stylized depiction of China's formal governance structure illustrates several key points about Chinese administration.

The first is its hierarchical nature, and the overlap between the party and the state apparatus. The second is the "one-level-down" supervision system, a common feature of the party and state organization. In this system, each level of government supervises its immediately subordinate level (e.g., the central government supervises the provinces; provinces supervise prefectures). The third is that, just as lower levels of government account for the majority of fiscal expenditures, they also employ the vast majority of China's civil servants.

One key point this graphic does not capture is the dual reporting relationships many local branches of functional agencies face: they are often subject to the immediately superior level of their functional agency for implementing technical standards, but most rely on local government officials for funding and personnel. These local officials often face different incentives and objectives from functional agencies, which can complicate the faithful enforcement of consistent standards.

# Appendix IV: Major Regular Events in the CCP Political Cycle and the National Five-Year Plan

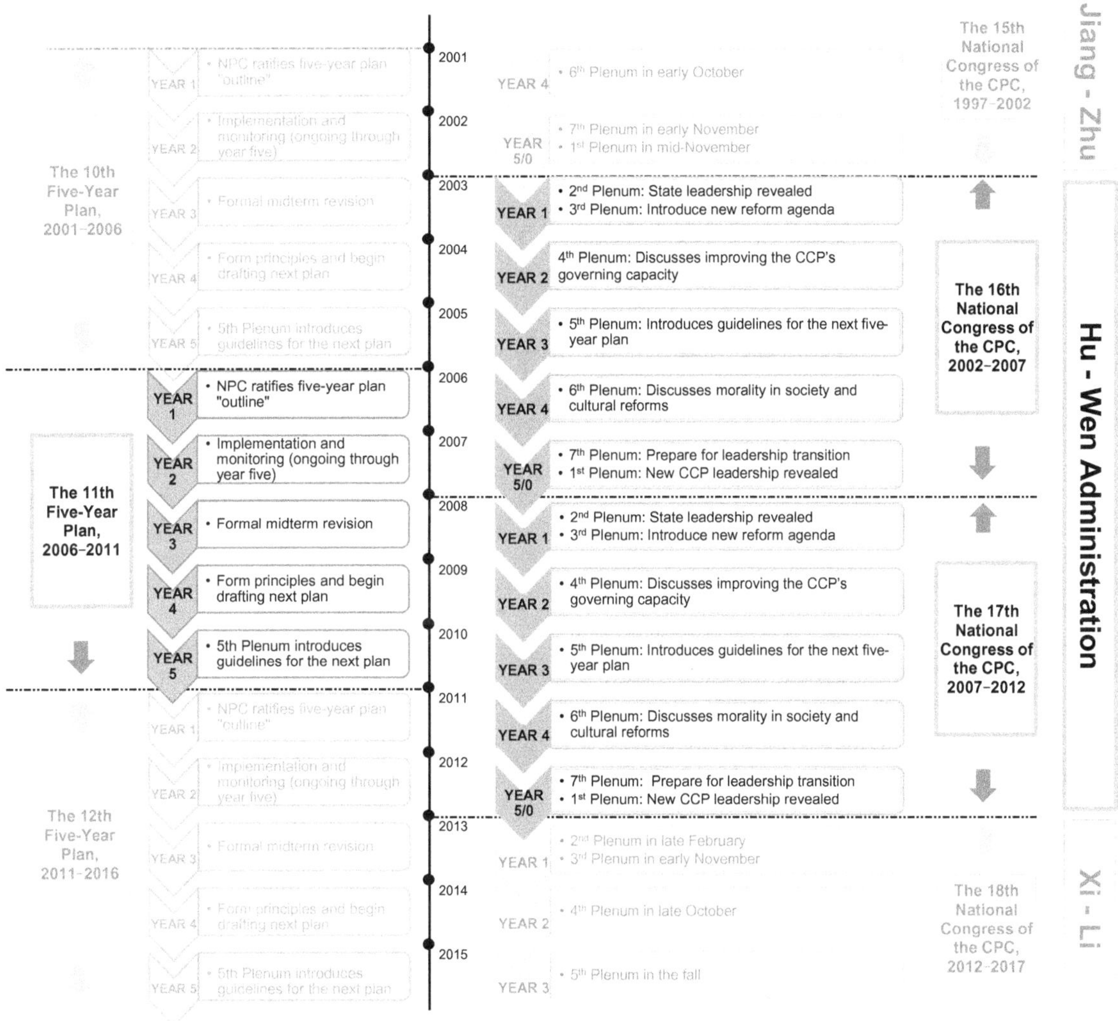

The graphic above illustrates two of the most important cycles in Chinese economic policymaking:

The left side shows the stages in which China's five-year plans are developed, approved, and implemented. While these plans have diminished in importance over the course of "reform and opening," they remain an important exercise in coordination across the breadth of the Chinese economic policymaking apparatus and have an important impact on investment patterns and priorities. The NDRC is responsible for coordinating the development of the five-year plan.[1]

The right side outlines the timing and general agendas of the Central Committee plenary sessions that take place regularly over the course of China's five- and ten-year leadership transition cycles. These plenary sessions are the most important regular party meetings outside the quinquennial national party congresses. Due to informal age limits, PBSC members are limited to a maximum of two five-year terms, though some serve only one.

The imperfect overlap of these two cycles is one source of inertia in China's economic policymaking process. For example, a new leadership team has the opportunity to lay out the reform agenda that will set the tone for its tenure at the Third Plenum. This is the first major CCP gathering following the completion of the full leadership transition process. However, even after the Third Plenum is complete and new leaders have put forward their agenda, their freedom of action is partially constrained by investment plans "baked-in" as part of the remaining two years of the current Five-Year Plan.

1. For more details on the five-year planning process see "China's 12th Five-Year Plan: How it actually works and what's in store for the next five years," APCO Worldwide, December 10, 2010.

# Appendix V: Key Meetings in China's Policymaking Calendar

| | | |
|---|---|---|
| Five-Year Meetings | National Congress of the Communist Party of China 中国共产党全国代表大会 | Leadership changes within the Communist Party take place at the National Congress, a gathering held every five years, usually in October or November. This is when the composition of the new PBSC is formally revealed for the first time. |
| | National Financial Work Conference 全国金融工作会议 (NFWC) | Held every five years (usually at the beginning of a year in which the NCCPC will be held), the National Financial Work Conference outlines the direction and objectives of financial reform for the five years to follow. The last conference was held in January 2012 under the leadership of the then premier Wen Jiabao and emphasized that the financial sector must "serve the real economy . . . and prevent overspeculation and virtual bubbles from inflating the economy." |
| Annual or Semiannual Meetings with Fixed Dates | National People's Congress 全国人民代表大会 (NPC) | The NPC is China's legislature, which meets in plenary session every year in the spring. This takes place alongside the annual meetings of the Chinese People's Political Consultative Conference, in a gathering referred to as China's "Two Meetings." This is when the annual growth target is announced, and the premier delivers the annual government work report. Outside of the annual plenary sessions, the smaller NPC standing committee exercises the authority of the NPC. It meets on a bimonthly basis. |
| | U.S.-China Strategic and Economic Dialogue 中美战略与经济对话 (S&ED) | The S&ED was established in April 2009 as an upgrade of the Strategic Economic Dialogue. It meets annually, usually around midyear, and its location alternates between Washington and Beijing. It is the highest-level regular bilateral dialogue between the United States and China. It contains both a Strategic Track and an Economic Track, the latter of which is chaired by the secretary of the treasury on the U.S. side and the vice premier with responsibility for foreign trade on the Chinese side. |

| | | |
|---|---|---|
| Annual or Semiannual Meetings with Fixed Dates | Beidaihe Summer Summit 北戴河会议 | The Beidaihe Summit takes places during the summer in Beidaihe, a coastal city and a summer resort in the province of Hebei. The attendance and content of the meetings vary with the preference of the current leadership generation. Under Xi, PBSC members (and some members of the Politburo) have used Beidaihe as a venue for informal private discussions regarding pressing policy issues and priorities for the coming year. |
| | Central Economic Work Conference 中央经济工作会议 (CEWC) | The Central Economic Work Conference is a joint party-state meeting held annually over two to three days in December. The meeting itself is closed to the press. The Work Conference sets priorities for economic reform for the coming year, and puts forward a key phrase to guide reform. The 2014 CEWC identified the "new normal" as the "main logic" for reform and the key phrase for 2015. |
| | U.S.-China Joint Commission on Commerce and Trade 中美商贸联合联委会 (JCCT) | The U.S.-China Joint Commission on Commerce and Trade (JCCT) is a bilateral dialogue held once a year in December. It is cochaired by the secretary of commerce and the U.S. trade representative on the U.S. side, and by the vice premier responsible for foreign trade on the Chinese side. In terms of substantive focus, the JCCT has significant overlap with the economic track of the S&ED, but is designed to focus more on the nuts and bolts of trade and investment-related issues. |
| | Central Fiscal Work Conference 全国财政工作会议 (CFWC) | Moderated and led by the minister of finance, the Central Fiscal Work Conference takes place at the end of every year following the Central Economic Work Conference. Its function is to evaluate the past fiscal year, and set the tone and agenda for fiscal policy in the upcoming year. |

| | | |
|---|---|---|
| Meetings without Fixed Dates | Plenary Sessions of the CCP Central Committee<br>中央委员会全体会议 | The Plenary Sessions of the Central Committee of the Community Party bring together the largest gathering of top party leaders outside the quinquennial CCP National Congresses. These meetings announce major policies, endorse key documents, and are generally among the most important events in China's policymaking calendar. At least one plenary session is held every year. Third Plenums in particular are noted for introducing a new leadership's reform agenda, a custom that dates back to the Third Plenum of the 11th CCP Central Committee in 1978, often referenced as the start of the "reform and opening" period. |
| | State Council Full Body Meeting<br>国务院全体会议 | The full 35-member State Council meets approximately every six months in plenary session. Outside of these meetings, the State Council executive committee exercises the authority of the full State Council. |
| | CFELSG<br>中央财经领导小组会议 | The regularity and relevance of CFELSG meetings have varied across generations of CCP leadership. Under Xi Jinping, the CFELSG has met nine times as of mid-February 2015 and, since its fifth meeting, enjoyed unusual publicity. Sections of subsequent meetings have even been shown on state television. These meetings have taken place approximately every two to three months. For further details, see Appendix II. |
| | CDRLSG<br>中央深化改革领导小组会议 | Established following the Third Plenary Session of the 18th National Congress, the CDRLSG has concluded nine meetings between its establishment at the end of 2014 and mid-February 2015. For more details, see Appendix I. |

| | | |
|---|---|---|
| | Politburo Study Sessions<br>中共中央政治局集体学习 | Since the 16th CCP National Congress, the CCP Politburo has held "group study sessions" on topics deemed to be of interest to the Party's top leaders. These events are attended by the full Politburo. They feature a guest lecturer delivering a carefully scripted presentation, followed by more free-form questions and answers between the Party leadership and the presenter. The 18th National Congress has held 20 group sessions as of mid-February 2015. Topics have ranged from anticorruption campaigns to the development of free-trade zones and from adherence to socialism to dialectical materialism. |
| Meetings without Fixed Dates | Politburo<br>中共中央政治局<br>and<br>Politburo Standing Committee<br>中共中央政治局常务会议<br>(PBSC) | The Politburo and the Politburo Standing Committee represent the top leadership of the CCP. The full Politburo meets roughly nine times annually, while the PBSC meets more frequently and exercises the full authority of the Politburo when the latter is not in session. Documents endorsed by the full Politburo carry more weight than those endorsed only by the PBSC, and documents endorsed by the full Central Committee are considered more authoritative still. |
| | State Council Executive Meeting<br>国务院常务会议 | The executive committee of the State Council meets on roughly a weekly basis, and exercises the authority of the State Council outside of its biannual plenary sessions. It functions as the State Council's primary decision-making body. Representatives from ministries are often invited to report or attend, depending on the matter under discussion. Meeting summaries are now regularly posted (complete with summary infographics) on the State Council website (http://english.gov.cn/). |

# About the Authors

**Matthew P. Goodman** is senior adviser for Asian economics and holds the William E. Simon Chair in Political Economy at CSIS. The Simon Chair examines current issues in international economic policy, with a focus on the Asia-Pacific region. Previously, he served as director for international economics on the National Security Council staff, working on the G-20, APEC, and other presidential summits. Before joining the White House, Goodman was senior adviser to the undersecretary for economic affairs at the U.S. Department of State. He has also worked at Albright Stonebridge Group, Goldman Sachs, and the U.S. Treasury Department. Goodman holds an M.A. from the Johns Hopkins School of Advanced International Studies and a B.Sc. from the London School of Economics.

**David A. Parker** is a research associate with the Simon Chair in Political Economy at CSIS. He manages research projects on Northeast Asian states' economic policy and policymaking and U.S. economic strategy toward the Asia-Pacific region. His current research interest is in Chinese, Japanese, and American economic strategies in the Asia Pacific. Parker is the coauthor of *China's Economic Policymaking at a Time of Transition* (CSIS, April 2014) and a contributing author of *Enhancing Value Chains: An Agenda for APEC* (CSIS, November 2013). He holds an M.A. in international economic relations from the School of International Service at American University with a concentration in international finance, a B.A. in Japan studies with a minor in economics from Tufts University, and studied at Doshisha University in Kyoto.

www.ingramcontent.com/pod-product-compliance
Lightning Source LLC
LaVergne TN
LVHW082353200926
848481LV00012B/3549